R
YEAR

Class\

Literacy

Julie Orrell

ıxt © Julie Orrell, 2003
Original illustrations © Nelson Thornes Ltd 2003

The right of Julie Orrell to be identified as author of this work has been asserted
by her in accordance with the Copyright, Designs and Patents Act 1988.

All rights reserved. The copyright holders authorise ONLY users of Classworks
Literacy Year R to make photocopies of the resource pages of this book for their
own or their students' immediate use within the teaching context. No other rights
are granted without permission in writing from the publishers or under licence from
the Copyright Licensing Agency Limited. Further details of such licences (for
reprographic reproduction) may be obtained from the Copyright Licensing Agency
Limited, of 90 Tottenham Court Road, London W1T 4LP.

Copy by any other means or for any other purpose is strictly prohibited without
prior written consent from the copyright holders. Application for such permission
should be addressed to the publishers.

Any person who commits any unauthorised act in relation to this publication may
be liable to criminal prosecution and civil claims for damages.

Published in 2003 by:
Nelson Thornes Ltd
Delta Place
27 Bath Road
CHELTENHAM
GL53 7TH
United Kingdom

03 04 05 06 07 / 10 9 8 7 6 5 4 3 2 1

A catalogue record for this book is available from the British Library

ISBN 0-7487-7320-7

Series based on an original idea by Paula Ross

Illustrations by Alex Machin
Page make-up by GreenGate Publishing Services, Tonbridge

Printed in Great Britain by Ashford Colour Press

CLASSWORKS – BLUEPRINTS – LEARNING TARGETS – LASTMINUTELESSON.CO.UK

Nelson Thornes publishes teacher's resource books packed with flexible ideas for use in primary schools. As well as *Classworks*, Nelson Thornes publishes *Blueprints* and *Learning Targets*, providing busy teachers with unbeatable curriculum coverage, inspiration and value for money. We mail teachers and schools about new Nelson Thornes publications regularly. To join the mailing list simply photocopy and complete the form below and return using the FREEPOST address to receive regular updates on our new and existing titles. Books can be bought by credit card over the telephone or internet. For more details log on to http://www.nelsonthornes.com or contact us on 01242 267 280. For FREE resources register at http://www.lastminutelesson.co.uk

---

Please add my name to the Nelson Thornes Teacher's Resources mailing list.

Mr/Mrs/Miss/Ms _____

Address _____

_____ Postcode _____

School address _____

_____ Postcode _____

To: Direct Marketing Coordinator, Nelson Thornes Ltd, FREEPOST SWC 0507, Cheltenham GL53 7ZZ

Acknowledgements

The author and publishers wish to thank the following for permission to use copyright material:

Six Dinner Sid by Inga Moore, reprinted by permission of Hodder & Stoughton Limited.

'Pass the Jam, Jim' by Kate Umansky and Margaret Chamberlain, reprinted by permission of The Random House Group.

The Happy Hedgehog Band by Martin Waddell and Jill Barton, reprinted by permission of Walker Books Limited.

'Little Miss Muffet' by Emma Chichester, reprinted by permission of Andersen Press Limited.

David Higham Associates for 'The Bug Chant' by Tony Mitton. 'The Bug Chant' © Tony Mitton.

Cover photo © Royalty-Free/CORBIS.

Every effort has been made to trace the copyright holders but if any have been inadvertently overlooked the publishers will be pleased to make the necessary arrangement at the first opportunity.

Contents

Unit	Outcome	Objectives	Page
Repetitive Patterns, Predictable Structures	A spoken musical story based on a shared text with patterned language	W2, W4, W10, W11; S2; T9, T13, T14	1
Counting Stories	A counting book using the pattern and structure of a shared text	W2, W4, W10; S3; T4, T7, T10, T13	13
Action Chants	A class action chant showcase	W1, W4; T10, T13, T14	26
Traditional Tales	A traditional tale, written as a group, plus mobile displays	W10; S1, S2; T2, T5 T7, T12, T13	37
Instructions	A set of instructions for planning a planning a party	W10, W11; S1; T11 T13, T15	48
Stories with a Pattern 1	A book using repetitive, patterned language, based on the structure of a shared text	W2, W4, W10, W11; S1, S4; T9, T13	64
Poems with Predictable Structures	A poem using the repeating structure of a shared text; individual poems for a poetry puzzle display	W1, W4; S4; T10, T12, T13, T14	74
Signs and Lists	Signs and lists for a class café role-play area	W11; T1, T11, T12, T13, T15	86
Nursery Rhymes	A class nursery rhyme display, based on *Humpty Dumpty*	W1, W4, W10; S1, S4; T10, T13, T14	98
Non-fiction: Recount	A recount of a visit	S1; T11, T13, T15	110
Stories with a Pattern 2	ICT sentences and labels using rhyme	W2, W4, W10, W11; S1, S4; T9, T13	122
Modern Poetry	An imaginative poem with an identified structure and rhyme pattern	W1, W4; T10, T13, T14	131
Instructions and Lists	A list poem based on a shared text	W10; S3; T11, T13, T15	144
Non-chronological reports	A non-chronological report – individual or group three-part zigzag book, based on a shared text	W11; S1; T1, T3, T11, T12, T13	156
Fairy Tales	A class book of stories retelling *The Three Billy-goats Gruff*	W10; S1, S2; T2, T5, T7, T12, T13	172

Introduction

How Classworks works

What this book contains

- Chunks of text, both annotated and 'blank' for your own annotations.

- Checklists (or toolkits), planning frames, storyboards, scaffolds and other writing aids.

- Examples of modelled, supported and demonstration writing.

- Lesson ideas including key questions and plenary support.

- Marking ladders for structured self-assessment.

- Blocked unit planning with suggested texts, objectives and outcomes.

- Word-level starter ideas to complement the daily teaching of phonics, handwriting and other skills.

- There are no scripts, no worksheets and nothing you can't change to suit your needs.

How this book is organised

- There are blocked units of work (see previous page) lasting different numbers of days, depending on the text type.

- Each blocked unit is organised into a series of chunks of teaching content.

- Each 'chunk' has accompanying checklists and other photocopiable resources.

- For every text we *suggest* annotations, checklists and marking ladders.

- Every unit follows the *teaching sequence for writing*, found in *Developing Early Writing* (DfES, 2000).

- You can mix and match teaching ideas, units and checklists as you see fit.

- The units have been designed to enable cross-curricular links across the six areas of learning of the Foundation Stage.

How you can use *Classworks* with your medium-term plan

- Refer to your medium-term planning for the blocking of NLS objectives and QCA Early Learning Goals.

- Find the text-type you want to teach (or just the objectives).

- Use the contents page to locate the relevant unit.

- Familiarise yourself with the text and language features using Classworks checklists and exemplar analysis pages, and resources such as *Developing Early Writing*.

- Browse the lesson ideas and photocopiables to find what you want to use.

- You can just use the text pages ... photocopy and adapt the checklists ... use or change some of the teaching ideas ... take whatever you want and adapt it to fit your class.

Planning a blocked unit of work with Classworks

Classworks units exemplify a blocked unit approach to planning the teaching of Literacy. What follows is an outline of this method of planning and teaching, and how *Classworks* can help you

You need: *Classworks* Literacy Year R, medium-term planning; OHT (optional).
Optional resources: your own choice of texts for extra analysis; *Developing Early Writing*.

Method

- From the medium-term planning, identify the **outcome**, **texts** and **objectives** you want to teach.

- *Classworks* units **exemplify** how some units could be planned, resourced and taught.

- Decide how to 'chunk' the text you are analysing, for example, introductory paragraph, paragraph 1, paragraph 2, closing paragraph.

- *Classworks* units give an example of **chunking** with accompanying resources and exemplar analysis. Texts for pupil analysis (labelled 'Pupil copymaster') are intended for whole class display on an OHT.

- **Whatever you think of the checklists provided, analyse the text with *your* class and build *your own* checklist for the whole text, and for each chunk.**

- Plan your blocked unit based on the following teaching sequence for writing.

- *Classworks* units outline one way of planning a **blocked unit**, with exemplifications of some days, and suggestions for teaching content on others.

Shared Reading – analysing the text – create 'checklist' or writer's toolkit	The children analyse another of that text type and add to checklist	Review checklist
Shared Writing – demonstrate application of 'checklist' to a small piece of writing	The children write independently based on your demonstration	Use examples on OHT to check against the 'checklist'

- This model is only a guideline, allowing the writing process to be scaffolded. You would want to build in opportunities for planning for writing, talking for writing, teaching explicit word-level and sentence-level objectives that would then be modelled in the shared writing, and so on. There are ideas for word-level and sentence-level starters in each lesson.

- Allow opportunities for the children to be familiar with the text type. This might include reading plenty of examples, drama, role play, video, and so on.

Assessment

- Make sure that 'checklists' are displayed around the room and referred to before writing and when assessing writing in the **plenary**.

- One or two children could work on an OHT, so their work could be the focus of the plenary.

- Use a **marking ladder** for the children to evaluate their writing. This is based on the checklist your class has built up. We give you an example of how it might look for each blocked unit. There's a blank copy on page 184.

What each page does

Text-type is written large at the top, and then on every page.

What a unit based on this material might look like.

Shaded sections refer to *Classworks* ideas, white sections to suggested extra content.

Text-based outcome clearly signalled.

Objectives spelt out.

Early learning goals listed

Word-level starter tag

Clear headings for each section of the page.

Main idea broken up into bullets and key questions.

Board-work examples highlighted clearly.

Child-friendly outcomes for every chunk of content.

***Classworks* resources referenced wherever relevant.**

Brief independent, pair or guided work idea.

Plenary guidance.

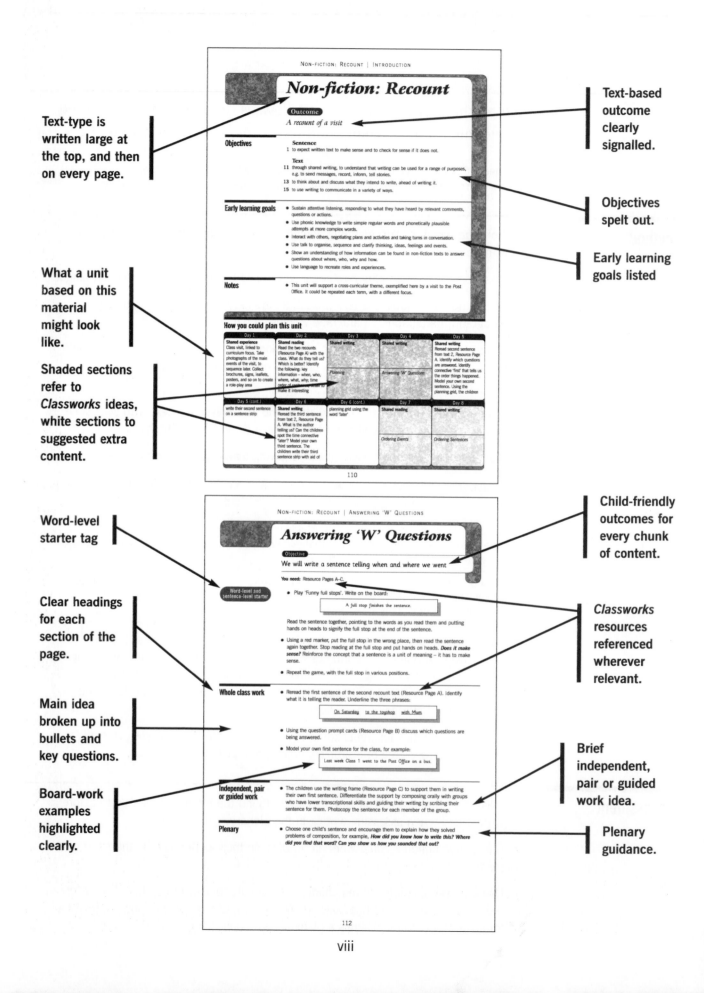

Repetitive Patterns, Predictable Structures

Outcome

A spoken musical story based on a shared text with patterned language

Objectives

Word

2 knowledge of grapheme/phoneme correspondences through identifying and writing initial and final phonemes in CVC words.

4 to link sound and spelling patterns by identifying alliteration in known and new and invented words.

10 [be taught] new words from their reading and shared experiences.

11 to make collections of personal interest or significant words and words linked to particular topics.

Sentence

2 to use awareness of the grammar of a sentence to predict words during shared reading and when rereading familiar stories.

Text

9 to be aware of story structures.

13 to think about and discuss what they intend to write, ahead of writing it.

14 to use experience of stories, poems and simple recounts as a basis for independent writing, e.g. retelling, substitution, extension, and through shared composition with adults.

Early learning goals

- Explore and experiment with words, sounds and texts.
- Hear and say initial and final sounds in words, and short vowel sounds within words.
- Use phonic knowledge to write simple regular words and phonetically plausible attempts at more complex words.
- Make up own stories, songs, rhymes and poems.
- Interact with others, negotiating plans and activities and taking turns in conversation.
- Enjoy listening to and using spoken and written language, and readily turn to it in play and learning.
- Listen with enjoyment, respond to and make up stories, songs and other music.
- Use language to recreate roles and experiences.

How you could plan this unit

Day 1	Day 1 (cont.)	Day 2	Day 3	Day 4
Shared reading Read *The Happy Hedgehog Band* (Resource Page A). Explore setting in first sentence. Discuss what Dickon Wood is like. Where is the wood? What do we see in woods? Describe the colours and sounds of the wood. How would you feel	if you were in the wood? List responses. Create a role-play area of Dickon Wood (or a local wood) with props to support final performance	**Talk for writing**	**Planning for writing**	**Shared writing**
		Word Rhythms	*Alliterative Names*	*A Story Start*

Day 5	Day 6	Day 7
Shared writing	**Shared writing** Model writing the last part of the story. Read the whole story with the class, review the writing and make word changes to improve the language. Fit the body rhythm patterns into the text and orally rehearse the performance	**Drama** Perform shared story for a school audience or video. Use drums for the rhythm, voice for the other noises and read the shared story that the class has written. Use props created for the role-play area
List Sentences		

Word Rhythms

Objective

We will explore the rhythm of words

You need: Resource Page A; a drum; other musical instruments.

Word-level starter

- Play 'Pass the sound'. With your class sitting in a circle, pass sounds around the circle. Each child listens to the child before and then copies the sound for the next child.

- Use a variety of sounds, including body rhythms, to reflect the phonemes that your class is learning in phonics work: clap, clap, clap / sssssssssss / hum / buzzzzzzzz / pop / click, click, click / tuwit tuwoo / mmmmmmm / clip clop, clip clop.

Whole class work

- Read *The Happy Hedgehog Band* (Resource Page A) with your class and identify the repeating rhythm:

> Tum tum te tum
> Diddle diddle dum
> Ratta tat tat
> BOOM

- Model how you can represent this rhythm in sound as well as in words. Clap out the rhythm and beat it on a drum.

- ***All words have a rhythm, and authors and poets often use the rhythm of words to make their writing fun to read.***

- Working in pairs, children explore the rhythm patterns of their first names, clapping out the beats. Support any children who find this concept hard by modelling their rhythm for them to copy.

- With your class, create a new rhythm pattern on a drum that can be used in your story, for example:

> Tum tum tum
> Dum diddle dum
> Boom boom boom
> CRASH!

- Model how you can record the pattern in words, so that you don't forget it.

Independent, pair or guided work

- Use the words from the text as a prompt to challenge the class to invent new rhythms using:

> hum   hoot   buzz   whistle   clap   click   pop

- In pairs, children use their voices and body rhythms to create new sound patterns for the animals in the wood.

Plenary

- Ask several pairs of children to demonstrate the rhythms that they have created.

- Challenge them to explain to the rest of the class why they chose their rhythm. ***Can it be improved?***

3

Alliterative Names

Objective

We will plan the characters for our performance

You need: Resource Page A (and enlarged version); thin A4 card (4 sheets).

Word-level starter

- Taking the example of 'Harry the happy hedgehog', challenge your class to tell you how the author has made this name sound fun (or good). Identify that it is the repeated initial sound 'h' that makes the name effective.

- Transfer the concept to investigate a new character for your shared story '... the rocking rabbit'. ***What is the first sound of 'rocking' and 'rabbit'?***

- Sitting in a circle, pass phoneme card r̲ around from child to child, encouraging them to say a word that starts with the sound when the card comes to them.

- Take suggestions of names that start with 'r' and decide with the class on a name to use in your story.

Whole class work

- Read *The Happy Hedgehog Band* again (Resource Page A) and explain: ***To plan our performance, we need to choose the characters for the story. Authors use story settings, like Dickon Wood, and characters to give detail to their story starts.***

- Use an enlarged copy of the text, and model how to highlight the names within the text: 'Harry', 'Helen', 'Norbert', 'Billy'. Identify that names start with a capital letter.

- Model writing a list of these four names.

- Start a new list with your chosen rabbit name. The children add their own suggestions of names in 'have a go' writing.

- Agree four character names for your story.

Independent, pair or guided work

- The children work in pairs to find names in the classroom book collection.

- A guided group writes the four chosen names on A4 name cards for the story characters.

Plenary

- Read out these names for the class and ask them to decide if each one is alliterative (thumbs up) or not alliterative (thumbs down):

Simone the slimy snake
Ricky the lonely mouse
Rupert the rocking rabbit
Harry the happy hedgehog
Henry the hot hippo
Clare the sad mole

- ***Can you invent any more alliterative names?***

A Story Start

Objective

We will write a shared story start, exploring setting and character

You need: Resource Pages A, D and E; a set of phoneme cards; art materials and thin card for making animal hat masks; drawing paper and crayons.

Word-level starter

- Give each child a phoneme card. Say the name of an animal for the class, stressing the first sound. If a child has the phoneme card to match the sound, they hold it up in the air. Everybody then makes the sound, followed by the animal word: 'rabbit', 'fox', 'dog', 'mole', 'hedgehog', 'deer', 'squirrel'.

Whole class work

- Read the first part of the story (Resource Page A), up to the word 'STOP!' Identify that this gives the story setting and main characters.

- Refer to your planned setting, planned rhythm and planned characters from previous lessons.

- Model writing a class version of the story start, using these ideas. Use the writing model (Resource Page D) as a prompt, adapting it to suit your class.

- When writing, explain the following points:
  - the story start tells us where it takes place, and who it is about
  - use of alliteration in the names
  - use of capital letters for names
  - the rhythm of the drums
  - use of noisy words (onomatopoeia)
  - the rhyme in 'humming' and 'drumming'
  - use of capital letters at the start of sentences
  - use of full stops at the end of sentences.

Independent, pair or guided work

- The children draw a picture of the wood in their story. Refer back to earlier discussions.

- In guided groups, the children make hat masks to represent the woodland creatures. Use this opportunity to develop their language of description – generate words to describe the animal's colour, texture, characteristics, movements and so on.

Plenary

- Using different story starts that are familiar to your class, challenge the children to guess which story belongs to the setting and characters. For example:

> Once upon a time, a little girl went to visit her granny in a cottage in the woods.
>
> Once upon a time, three goats lived in a grassy field.
>
> Deep in the heart of Dickon Wood, lived a happy hedgehog named Harry.

- Draw up a class checklist for story starts (see Resource Page E for ideas).

List Sentences

Objective

We will make a 'list sentence' joined by the word 'and'

You need: Resource Pages A–E; magnetic letters; scissors.

Word-level starter

- Use magnetic letters to make the word 'and' on the board. Sound out the three phonemes in the word, holding up one finger to represent each phoneme that the children hear.

- *'And' is a really useful word to be able to read and spell, as it is used a lot in reading and writing.*

- Tell your class that you are going to try to trick them by muddling the letters. Their challenge is to talk with their partner and work out what is wrong.

- Muddle the word in different combinations, one at a time, for the class to solve:

| dan | and | dna | nad | an | na | dn | and |

Whole class work

- Read the story on Resource Page A with your class.

- Focus on the 'list sentence' in paragraph 5 and identify the connective 'and'.

- In pairs, the children make oral lists of animals, linked by 'and'.

- Model how to write a new version of the middle section, referring to Resource Page D but adapting it to include suggestions from the class.

- Explain the following points as you write:
  - the repeating rhythm refrain
  - the long list sentence, with the animals linked by the connective 'and'
  - the noisy words (onomatopoeia)
  - the use of capital letters for 'STOP!', to tell the reader to shout it out
  - the use of punctuation to help the reader to read the story correctly.

Independent, pair or guided work

- The children explore assembling the woodland animals in a list sentence, starting with 'STOP! cried...' and separated by 'and'.

- Using the animal name cards (Resource Page B) and connective words (Resource Page C), the children cut and stick their own list sentence.

Plenary

- In pairs, the children read their own sentence to their response partner. Partners check that the sentence makes sense.

- Add to the class checklist the key features of the middle of the story (see Resource Page E for ideas).

Exemplar material

The Happy Hedgehog Band

Deep in the heart of Dickon Wood lived a happy hedgehog named Harry. Harry loved noise so he made a big drum and he banged on the drum tum-tum-te-tum.

A hedgehog called Helen was out in the wood. She heard tum-tum-te-tum and she liked it. So she made a drum and went off to join in the drumming. And so did a hedgehog named Norbert and another called Billy; they both made drums and followed the tum-tum-te-tums, until all of the hedgehogs with drums were gathered together at Harry's. Tum-tum-te-tum went one drum; that was Harry. Diddle-diddle-dum went one drum; that was Helen. Ratta-tat-tat went one drum; that was Norbert.

And BOOM went one drum; that was Billy.

Tum-tum-te-tum diddle-diddle-dum ratta-tat-tat BOOM. Tum-tum-te-tum diddle-diddle-dum ratta-tat-tat BOOM.

The whole wood was humming and tumming and drumming. "STOP!" cried the pheasant, the owl and the bee, the mole from his hole and a badger called Sam and his mother, and the fox and the crow, the deer and the dove, the frog and the toad and the spider and the dog who was lost in the wood. Tum went the band and they STOPPED! "We want to play too!" said the others. "But we haven't got drums. So what can we do?" And nobody knew except Harry.

Harry knew all about noise. So he said, "You can hum, you can hoot, you can buzz, you can whistle, you can clap, you can click, you can pop. We'll carry on with the drums."

And … they did.

And the dog who was lost in the wood just danced.

Martin Waddell

(Pupil copymaster)

Animal name cards

the mole	the badger
the crow	the deer
the toad	the fox
the bee	the owl
the frog	the dog who was lost in the wood

PHOTOCOPIABLE · PHOTOCOPIABLE ·

(Pupil copymaster)

Connectives

and	and
and	and
and	and
Stop! cried	.
and	and

Exemplar material

Modelled writing

Deep in the heart of Willow Wood lived a rocking rabbit named Ronald.

Ronald loved making rhythms on his big woodland drum.

Tum tum tum went Ronald's drum.

Rebecca the rabbit joined in. Dum diddle dum.

Reg the rabbit made a drum. Boom boom boom.

Ruby rabbit followed the drums. Crash!

The whole wood was humming and drumming.

Tum tum tum, dum diddle dum, boom boom boom, crash!

STOP! cried the badger and the fox and the mole and the deer and the frog and the toad.

The rocking rabbit band stopped.

"We want to play too! said the others, but we haven't got drums"

Ronald told the animals what to do.

"You can clap, you can whistle, you can hoot, you can pop, you can hum, you can buzz!"

And ... [ADD NOISES] they did.

And the dog who was lost in the wood just danced.

Classworks Literacy Year R © Julie Orrell, Nelson Thornes Ltd 2003

(Exemplar material)

Checklist for a patterned story

Story start

- Where is the story set?

- Who are the main characters?

- Start by telling the reader when or where

- Alliteration for the characters' names

Story middle

- Repeat the rhythm

- Make something happen!

- Use capital letters to SHOUT noisy words

- Use a list sentence joined with 'and' to give a different rhythm

Story end

- Repeat the pattern 'You can...'

- Use ... to create suspense – make the reader wonder what happens next

- Give it an unexpected quiet ending after all the noise!

Marking ladder

In Foundation Stage Reception, work is likely to be assessed orally with the child, at the point of writing. The features identified as a checklist can be used to provide a focus and any comments recorded as a marking ladder.

Name: _____

Tick		Comment
	I can describe the wood.	
	I can make a rhythm.	
	I can use alliteration.	
	I can spell the word 'and'.	
	I can use noisy words.	

Counting Stories

Outcome

A counting book using the pattern and structure of a shared text

Objectives

Word

2 knowledge of grapheme/phoneme correspondences through identifying and writing initial and final phonemes in CVC words.

4 to link sound and spelling patterns by identifying alliteration in known and new and invented words.

10 [be taught] new words from their reading and shared experiences.

Sentence

3 [be taught] that words are ordered left to right and need to be read that way to make sense.

Text

4 to compare 'told' versions with what the book 'says'.

7 to use knowledge of familiar texts to re-enact or retell to others, recounting the main points in correct sequence.

10 to reread and recite stories and rhymes with predictable and repeated patterns and experiment with similar rhyming patterns.

13 to think about and discuss what they intend to write, ahead of writing it.

Early learning goals

- Explore and experiment with words, sounds and texts.
- Hear and say initial and final sounds in words, and short vowel sounds within words.
- Continue a rhyming string.
- Use phonic knowledge to write simple regular words and phonetically plausible attempts at more complex words.
- Make up own stories, songs, rhymes and poems.
- Know that print carries meaning and that English is read left to right and top to bottom.

How you could plan this unit

Day 1	Day 1 (cont.)	Day 2	Day 3	Day 4
Experience Discuss what a nursery rhyme is and what it is for. Ask the children for examples. Recite a selection: *Little Bo Peep*, *Little Jack Horner*, *Old Mother Hubbard*. Point to use of 'little' and 'old' in	names. Record individual and group performances	**Talk and drama for writing**	**Planning for writing**	**Shared reading**
		Traditional Rhymes	*Number Names*	*Making Rhymes*

Day 5	Day 6	Day 6 (cont.)
Shared writing	**Writing** Publish class book. Guided groups use computer to print texts 1–10 on writing frame template, using the same font. Enlarge to A3. In pairs, the children illustrate pages. Put pages in number order and make	a cover with details of title, authors, publisher
Writing Verses		

Traditional Rhymes

Objective

We will learn and think about the nursery rhyme *Little Miss Muffet*

You need: Resource Pages A and G; dressing-up clothes; large plastic spider on a string; large sheet of paper for checklist.

Word-level starter

- Recite the traditional nursery rhyme *Little Miss Muffet* (Resource Page A).

- Investigate the new and unusual words from the rhyme: 'tuffet', 'curds', 'whey'. Ask for suggestions as to what would make sense in the context of each word.

> ### DICTIONARY DEFINITIONS
>
> tuffet = a) a tuft of grass; b) through misunderstanding of the nursery rhyme, a small stool
>
> curds = the solid part of soured milk that cheese is made from
>
> whey = the thin, watery part of soured milk

The dictionary tells us that the nursery rhyme has got it wrong, that a tuffet should really be a tuft of grass. Here is an example of how spoken language becomes part of our culture and the dictionary changes to include it.

Whole class work

- Experiment with missing out the last words from each line of the rhyme and challenge the children to complete them.

- Recite the nursery rhyme together, while two children act out the rhyme.

- Challenge your class to imagine another creature coming along to sit down beside Miss Muffet. **What could it be, and why?**

- With response partners, the children invent different scenarios.

Independent, pair or guided work

- The children work in small groups to think of a scenario to act out for the rest of the class to guess. **What is sitting down beside Miss Muffet and what happens next?**

- Use dressing-up clothes and props for each group in turn to act out their scenario. Props can also act as stimulus for the discussion.

Plenary

- Review the drama with your class, telling them which bits stood out for you ('golden moments'), and explain why.

- Encourage the children to talk to a partner and to tell each other what they liked best, and why.

- Start a checklist with the class (see Resource Page G for ideas) recording what they have discovered so far – that nursery rhymes use old-fashioned and unusual words and that characters often have 'Little' or 'Old' as part of their names, which helps to describe them.

Number Names

Objective

We will understand how counting stories work

You need: Resource Pages B, C (enlarged and individual) and G; examples of counting stories and rhymes; large plastic carrier bag; Blu-tack™; whiteboards.

Word-level starter

- Explain that you are going to try to trick the class with some number words. *You are going to get a clue through the first phoneme in the word but then you have to guess the rest of the word.* Point out that it will be especially tricky for 'four'/'five', 'six'/'seven' and 'two'/'ten' because these start with the same sound.

- Put the number cards (Resource Page C) in a bag and draw them out one by one, showing only the left-hand side and pointing out and making the first sound. NB The numbers one (*w*) and eight (*ay*) have unusual spelling representations – make sure you use the sound not the letter.

- Challenge the children to guess which number word from one to ten you have chosen, and to show you by holding up fingers to represent the number. The children check their answer with a partner, ensuring it starts with the right sound.

Whole class work

- Read the poem *Little Miss Muffet Counts to Ten* (Resource Page B). Challenge the children to tell you what sort of story it is. Responses will vary, but focus on the counting aspect – how each verse has an increasing number from one to ten.

- Give the children a chance to think of any other counting stories or rhymes that work in the same way.

- Discuss the difference between numerals and words, referring to class displays.

- Read the number cards for numbers four and five again, pointing out both the numeral and the word to represent it.

- *Write your age on your whiteboards.* Discuss how a numeral is a quicker way of representing the name of a number.

- Model for your class how to put the number cards in ascending order.

- Model how you are going to use the numerals to number the ten pages of the writing frame to make sure that the new class book has the right number of pages.

Independent, pair or guided work

- Differentiate the number matching activity according to ability:
  a) ordering the complete cards (support through numeral, word and pictures)
  b) matching the numeral half of the cards to the word and picture half
  c) giving only the word half and asking the group to draw the numeral or pictures

Plenary

- Say number words one at a time, giving only the sound of first phoneme – <u>w</u> (one); <u>t</u> (two); <u>th</u> (three); <u>f</u> (four); <u>f</u> (five); <u>s</u> (six); <u>s</u> (seven); <u>ay</u> (eight); <u>n</u> (nine); <u>t</u> (ten). Do this in random order and challenge the class to work out the number you are thinking of.

- Add to the class checklist: 'This counting story starts with number one and ascends, in order, to ten.' (See also Resource Page G.)

Making Rhymes

Objective

We will plan rhyming words for a new page of our story

You need: Resource Pages B, D and E; plastic spider attached to a very long piece of string; Blu-tack™.

Word-level starter

- Play the 'Pass the spider' game to generate a rhyme string for the word 'whey'. Hold on to the loose end of the string, and pass the spider around the circle, generating rhymes as you go. Prompt contributions as needed by running through rhymes as examples:

> hay … may … sleigh … day … bay … grey … way … they …

- *How far around the circle will the spider's rhyme thread stretch?*

- Scribe the rhymes that the class have generated on the board.

Whole class work

- Reread *Little Miss Muffet Counts to Ten* (Resource Page B) and stress the last word of every verse.

- After several verses, ask if anyone has noticed something interesting about the last word of every verse. Identify that the words all rhyme with 'whey' – just like in the 'Pass the spider' game.

- Together, look at the words that the author has chosen at the end of verses, and identify any that the class came up with in the spider game.

- Make a word bank of words that rhyme with 'whey' and add any new ones (see Resource Page D).

- *Now we have made a new rhyme for the last line, we need new words for lines 4 and 5.* Explore the pattern of lines 4 and 5 in several of the verses and identify that they introduce another animal and they also rhyme with each other.

- Stick the rhyme pair cards (Resource Page E) on the board with Blu-tack™ and model how you can match them with other rhyme cards. *This is what the author has done to make new lines.*

- Add to the class checklist: 'Lines 4 and 5 rhyme; line 6 rhymes with "whey".'

Independent, pair or guided work

- Divide your class into ten groups and give each group a rhyme pair card.

- Using the cards as a prompt, the children draw a picture to show their chosen animal and rhyming word.

Plenary

- Sing *There's a fox in a box* and invent new verses with animal rhymes, for example, "There's a cat in a hat", "There's a mole in a hole", "There are llamas in pyjamas".

> There's a fox in a box
> in my little house
> My little house, my little house.
> There's a fox in a box in my little house
> And there isn't much room for
> ME!

Writing Verses

Objective

We will write a new class big book of a counting story

You need: Resource Pages F (10 copies plus one enlarged) and G; whiteboards; plasticine.

Word-level starter

- Call out words one at a time, challenging the class to write the first sound they can hear on their whiteboards: 'dragon', 'wagon', 'cat', 'hat', 'dog', 'log', 'fish', 'dish'.

Whole class work

- Using a blank enlarged writing frame (Resource Page F), model how to use planned rhyming words to make a new verse of the counting book.

- *The first part has been written for us, because it doesn't change:*

> Little Miss Muffet
> Sat on a tuffet
> Eating her curds and whey,

- *At the end of line 4 there is an empty word space, 'When along came ...' and in that space we need to put our number and rhyming animal, as the author does:*

> When along came four dragons

- *At the end of line 5 we need to put in our animal's rhyming word:*

> With bright painted wagons

- *We need to invent a new line 6 that ends with a word to rhyme with 'whey':*

> And bales of freshly mown hay.

- Divide the class into ten groups, as in the previous lesson, and ask them to discuss with their partners what their finished verse will be.

- Draw attention to the class checklist for the counting story (see Resource Page G).

Independent, pair or guided work

- With your assistant work with each group in turn, discussing the composition and helping the children to modify their work if needed, referring to the class checklist.

- Number the 10 copies of the writing frame and scribe each group composition on to a frame, modelling writing as you do so. Explain how you are leaving finger spaces between words and point out the number and rhyming words for the group.

- The children waiting for guided input can make plasticine spiders to sing along with the plenary.

Plenary

- Sing and enjoy the newly composed verses as a class, in numerical order.

- *Which verse had the funniest rhyme? Which verse had the cleverest rhyme?* The children vote with thumbs up for their favourites.

Pupil copymaster

A traditional nursery rhyme

Little Miss Muffet
Sat on a tuffet,
Eating her curds and whey,
When along came a spider
Who sat down beside her,
And frightened Miss Muffet away!

(Exemplar material)

Little Miss Muffet Counts to Ten

Little Miss Muffet
Sat on a tuffet,
Eating her curds and whey,
When along came a spider
Who sat down beside her,
And said to Miss Muffet, "Please stay!"

Little Miss Muffet
Sat on a tuffet,
Eating her curds and whey,
When along came two lemurs
With trumpets and streamers,
And bunting to make a display.

Little Miss Muffet
Sat on a tuffet,
Eating her curds and whey,
When along came three magpies
With taffeta bow-ties
And waistcoats of very pale grey.

Little Miss Muffet
Sat on a tuffet,
Eating her curds and whey,
When along came four foxes
With neatly wrapped boxes,
And jellies lined up on a sleigh.

Little Miss Muffet
Sat on a tuffet,
Eating her curds and whey,
When along came five pussycats
With milkshakes and party hats
And pots of chocolate soufflé.

Little Miss Muffet
Sat on a tuffet,
Eating her curds and whey,
When along came six poodles
With oodles of noodles
And flutes which they started to play.

Little Miss Muffet
Sat on a tuffet,
Eating her curds and whey,
When along came seven bears
With a table and chairs.
They said, "We'll sit here, if we may."

Little Miss Muffet
Sat on a tuffet,
Eating her curds and whey,
When along came eight puffins
With blueberry muffins,
And each clutched a tiny bouquet.

Little Miss Muffet
Sat on a tuffet,
Eating her curds and whey,
When along came nine gibbons
With balloons tied to ribbons,
And bananas arranged on a tray.

Little Miss Muffet
Sat on a tuffet,
Eating her curds and whey,
When along came ten crocodiles
With a box and ten greedy smiles.
They saw her and shouted "Hooray!"

There was cheering and prancing,
And whooping and dancing –
And what did the crocodiles say?
"You have made a mistake:
We have brought you a cake!
Don't you know? It's your birthday
today!"

Emma Chichester Clark

PHOTOCOPIABLE · PHOTOCOPIABLE

Pupil copymaster

Counting frame

one	☆	1
two	☆☆	2
three	☆☆☆	3
four	☆☆☆☆	4
five	☆☆☆☆☆	5
six	☆☆☆☆☆☆	6
seven	☆☆☆☆☆☆☆	7
eight	☆☆☆☆☆☆☆☆	8
nine	☆☆☆☆☆☆☆☆☆	9
ten	☆☆☆☆☆☆☆☆☆☆	10

Classworks Literacy Year R © Julie Orrell, Nelson Thornes Ltd 2003

Pupil copymaster

Words that rhyme with 'whey'

day	play
hooray	sleigh
tray	say
grey	Hey!
weigh	neigh

Pupil copymaster

Rhyme pairs

cats	hats
dragons	wagons
dogs	logs
llamas	pyjamas
foxes	boxes
fishes	dishes
hens	pens
pigs	twigs
frogs	logs
snakes	cakes

Pupil copymaster

Writing frame

Little Miss Muffet

Sat on a tuffet,

Eating her curds and whey,

When along came _____

With _____

And _____

PHOTOCOPIABLE · PHOTOCOPIABLE

(Exemplar material)

Checklist for counting stories

- Uses unusual words

- Uses names that start with 'Little' or 'Old'

- Lines 4 and 5 need to rhyme

- Line 6 needs to rhyme with 'whey'

- The numbers on pages rise from 1 to 10

(**Marking ladder**)

In Foundation Stage Reception, work is likely to be assessed orally with the child, at the point of writing. The features identified as a checklist can be used to provide a focus and any comments recorded as a marking ladder.

Name: _____

Tick		Comment
	We planned our new sentences.	
	We made lines 4 and 5 rhyme.	
	We found a rhyme for 'whey'.	
	We can read our new page.	
	We put our page in number order.	
	I can read my sentence back.	
	We typed and printed our work.	

Action Chants

Outcome

A class action chant showcase

Objectives

Word

1 to understand and be able to rhyme through: recognising, exploring and working with rhyming patterns; extending these patterns by analogy, generating new and invented words in speech and spelling.

4 to link sound and spelling patterns by using knowledge of rhyme to identify families of rhyming CVC words.

Text

10 to reread and recite stories and rhymes with predictable and repeated patterns and experiment with similar rhyming patterns.

13 to think about and discuss what they intend to write, ahead of writing it.

14 to use experience of stories, poems and simple recounts as a basis for independent writing, e.g. retelling, substitution, extension and through shared composition with adults.

Early learning goals

● Explore and experiment with words, sounds and texts.

● Use phonic knowledge to write simple regular words and phonetically plausible attempts at more complex words.

● Hear and say initial and final sounds in words, and short vowel sounds within words.

● Enjoy listening to and using spoken and written language, and readily turn to it in their play and learning.

● Listen with enjoyment and respond to rhymes and make up their own rhymes.

How you could plan this unit

Day 1	Day 1 (cont.)	Day 2	Day 3	Day 4
Personal experience Discuss how chants have been used by children for centuries to provide a rhythm when they are playing. Repeat the old chants and rhymes on Resource Page A. Use balls or skipping hoops to demonstrate how chants	help provide a rhythm. The children ask older relatives for any playground chants they can remember	**Shared reading**	**Shared reading**	**Shared writing**
		Responding to Rhythm	*Rhyme Strings*	*Writing Rhymes*

Day 5	Day 6	Day 6 (cont.)
Shared writing, speaking and listening	**Chant showcase** Invite pairs of older children, parents and grandparents to perform the chants they used for playground games. Present the new class version of *The Bug Chant*, with the children clapping/ demonstrating the	movements/using percussion
Using Adjectives		

26

Responding to Rhythm

Objective

We will listen and respond to the rhythm of a chant

You need: Resource Page B; phoneme cards; highlighter pen; percussion instruments; plasticine; pipe cleaners.

- Give a phoneme card to each pair of children and ask them to discuss which sound is on their card. Provide support if needed to identify the sounds: b̲, u̲, g̲, r̲, e̲, d̲, m̲, a̲, n̲, t̲, h̲, p̲, s̲.

- *We are going to use the sounds to make some human words. Listen very carefully to see if your sound is in the word. If you can hear your sound, hold up your card.*

- Investigate the words one at a time. Check that the sounds are right by sounding out the word with your class, stressing each phoneme. The children with the listed sounds stand together to make the word (CVC word-building).

  Words to build:

bug	bugs	rug	man	mat	red	bed	mug	hat	pat

Whole class work

- Read the extract from *The Bug Chant* (Resource Page B) with your class.

- Model the rhythm of the chant by moving your head from side to side as you read.

- Explain that the chant needs the rhythm to make it work – rhythm is important. (The rhythm works on a 1212222212 pattern, stressing the 1st, 3rd and 9th beat or syllable in each verse.) The chant works because the pattern stays the same.

- Use a highlighter pen and highlight these words/beats on the shared text.

- Reread the chant and encourage your class to join in, responding to the beat by clapping or nodding.

- Use a variety of percussion instruments to develop awareness of the chant's rhythm.

Independent, pair or guided work

- The children use plasticine and pipe cleaners to make their own bug models. Guide their work by asking questions, *What sort of bug is it? Tell me about the colours of the bug. Where does your bug live? What does your bug do?*

Plenary

- Do the 'Bug Dance'. Reread the chant with your class. The children make their bugs 'dance' to the rhythm.

Rhyme Strings

Objective

We will look for rhyme patterns and make a rhyme string

You need: Resource Page B; toy cat; magnetic letters; whiteboards (one between two).

Word-level starter

- Using the word 'cat', pass a toy cat around the circle, generating rhymes.

- Investigate rhyme generation by changing the first phoneme of the word 'cat'. Using magnetic letters, put the letters 'a' and 't' on the whiteboard.

- Model how you can generate rhyming words by adding a different initial sound: 'cat', 'bat', 'mat', 'sat', 'hat', 'pat', 'rat'.

- List the resulting words to exemplify a rhyme string.

Whole class work

- Reread *The Bug Chant* (Resource Page B), encouraging the children to join in with the actions and words.

- Challenge the children to tell you what is different about the words that appear as a strong beat in the rhythm by stressing them. Identify that the words rhyme.

- ***In the last verse, the poet asks us to make up some bugs of our own. Our challenge is to use the poet's rhyme and rhythm pattern and make up two new verses of our own. To do this, we need to make a string of words that rhyme that we can use in the chant.***

- Refer back to the word-level work on generating rhyme strings.

Independent, pair or guided work

- Model how to write the word 'cat', sounding out each phoneme as you write it.

- In pairs, the children use whiteboards to write the three phonemes.

- Show how to rub out the first sound <u>c</u> and encourage the children to investigate putting a different sound at the front to make a new word. Support those with weak transcription skills by guiding their word-building using magnetic letters or letter tiles.

- When a new word has been generated, the children check with their response partner that it is a word. Each child writes it on the flip chart to make a list of words that rhyme with 'cat'.

Plenary

- ***Do these words rhyme with 'cat'?*** The children vote using thumbs up/thumbs down as you say the following words. Allow time for them to repeat the word to themselves to see if it rhymes.

mat	man	rat	fat	dog
sat	hat	bat	pen	cat

28

Writing Rhymes

Objective

We will make up a new verse using the pattern of rhythm and rhyme

You need: Resource Page C; postcard-sized pieces of card; magnetic letters; art materials.

Word-level starter

- Generate a rhyme string using the word 'mad'. Record the words generated on individual pieces of card, in planning for the independent task – 'mad', 'sad', 'dad', 'lad', 'pad'.

Whole class work

- Refer back to the rhyme string generated in the previous lesson and recorded on the flip chart. *We now need to choose two or three of these rhymes to put into our new chant.*

- *First we need to choose a noun, a 'thing' for the last line.* Agree which noun you will use – 'cat', 'rat', 'bat', 'hat' or 'mat'.

- *Now we need to choose two words to describe the bug, the second one needs to rhyme with our noun.* For example you could choose 'fat'.

- *We need to choose a noun from our rhyme string, for the bugs to sit on.* Agree another noun – 'rat', 'cat', 'bat', 'mat' or 'hat'.

- Model selecting words from the rhyme string and inserting them into the writing frame (Resource Page C) to make a new verse:

> Round bugs, fat bugs,
>
> sitting on my cat bugs.

- Read the new verse aloud, checking that it follows the rhythm of the chant.

Independent, pair or guided work

- Using the rhyme cards generated in word-level work, the children work in guided groups to make a new verse, for example,

> Mad bugs, sad bugs,
>
> hopping on my dad bugs.

- Groups working independently use magnetic letters or the phoneme cards <u>c</u> <u>a</u> <u>t</u> to try to make the word 'cat' and then draw a picture of a bug sitting on their cat.

Plenary

- Read the new version of the chant, including the newly composed verses. Check that they follow the pattern of rhythm and rhyme by speaking the chant together and stressing the key words.

Using Adjectives

Objective

We will use adjectives to describe our bugs

You need: Resource Pages B and D; pieces of card; Blu-tack™; tape recorder.

Word-level starter

- Play 'The adjective game'. The children close their eyes and listen as you give them a noun to think about. Encourage them to think of adjectives to describe the different noun-starters, using their senses of look, taste, feel and smell, to paint a picture of what they can see in their imaginations.

| flower | egg | fish | animal |

- After each adjective game, ask several children to describe their noun.

- *Adjectives make words much more interesting. This is a trick that writers use.*

Whole class work

- Look at *The Bug Chant* (Resource Page B) again and explain that you are going to hunt for adjectives, or describing words. Ask the children to raise their hands when they hear a word that describes a bug.

- Model how you can write the adjectives on cards, to use as a word bank. Stick the adjective cards to the board with Blu-tack™.

- Ask the children if they can read any of the word cards, reminding them to look at the first sound to give them a clue. Ask any children who correctly identify one of the words to explain to the class how they knew that it was right, exemplifying their decoding strategies.

Independent, pair or guided work

- Groups each tape record a verse of the chant, stressing the rhythm as they read. This builds towards a class compilation recording.

- The children working independently draw a picture on bug-shaped paper of their favourite bug (or colour in the bug on Resource Page D), using 'have a go' writing to write words underneath to describe their bug. Words from the adjective collection on the board can provide a word bank as needed.

Plenary

- The children close their eyes, sit with their hands up, listening carefully as you describe a member of the class using a range of increasingly specific descriptions. Each child puts their hand down when they hear a description that doesn't apply to them, leaving one child with their hand up at the end.

(**Exemplar material**)

Old-fashioned rhymes

One, two, three, four, five,
Once I caught a fish alive,
Six, seven, eight, nine, ten,
Then I let it go again.
Why did you let it go?
Because it bit my finger so.
Which finger did it bite?
This little finger on the right.

Pat-a-cake, pat-a-cake, baker's man,
Bake me a cake as fast as you can;
Pat it and prick it, and mark it with B,
Put it in the oven for baby and me.

Inky pinky ponky,
my daddy saw a donkey,
the donkey died,
daddy cried,
inky pinky ponky.

One, two,
Buckle my shoe;
Three, four,
Knock at the door;
Five, six
Pick up sticks;
Seven, eight,
Lay them straight;
Nine, ten,
A big fat hen.

(**Pupil copymaster**)

The Bug Chant

Red bugs, bed bugs,
find them on your head bugs.
Green bugs, mean bugs,
lanky, long, lean bugs.
Pink bugs, sink bugs,
swimming in your drink bugs.
Smooth bugs, hairy bugs,
flying like a fairy bugs.
Fierce bugs, tame bugs,
some without a name bugs.
Whine bugs, drone bugs,
Write some of your own bugs.
Bzzzzzzzzzzzzzzzz ...

from The Bug Chant, *by Tony Mitton*

Classworks Literacy Year R © Julie Orrell, Nelson Thornes Ltd 2003

(**Pupil copymaster**)

The Bug Chant – writing frame

BY CLASS _____

Red bugs, bed bugs,
find them on your head bugs.
Green bugs, mean bugs,
lanky, long, lean bugs.
Pink bugs, sink bugs,
swimming in your drink bugs.
Smooth bugs, hairy bugs,
flying like a fairy bugs.
Fierce bugs, tame bugs,
some without a name bugs.
Whine bugs, drone bugs,
Write some of your own bugs.

_____ bugs, _____ bugs,

sitting on my _____ bugs.

_____ bugs, _____ bugs,

dancing on my _____ bugs.

Bzzzzzzzzzzzzzzzz ...

based on The Bug Chant, *by Tony Mitton*

PHOTOCOPIABLE · PHOTOCOPIABLE ·

Pupil copymaster

My bug, by _____

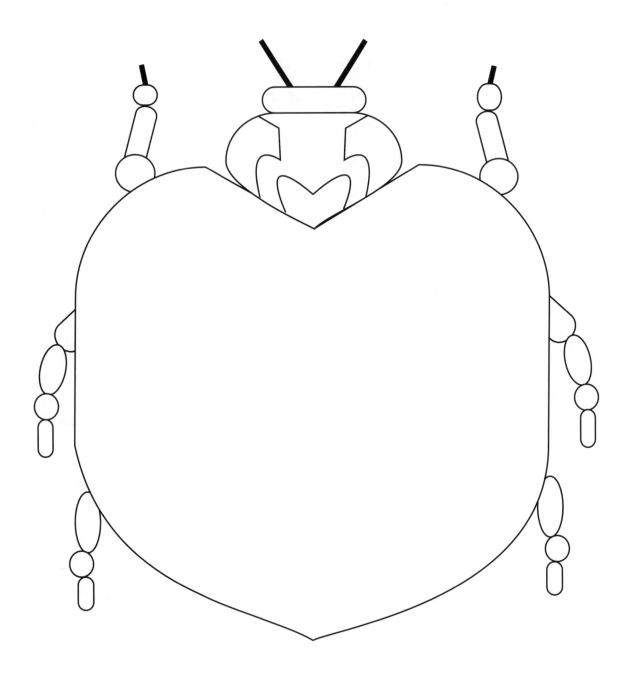

Classworks Literacy Year R © Julie Orrell, Nelson Thornes Ltd 2003

(Exemplar material)

Checklist for action chants

- They are good for playground games

- They have a repeating rhythm

- They have a rhyme pattern

- The rhythm and rhyme patterns may be the same

- They are fun to say out loud!

(**Marking ladder**)

In Foundation Stage Reception, work is likely to be assessed orally with the child, at the point of writing. The features identified as a checklist can be used to provide a focus and any comments recorded as a marking ladder.

Name: _____

Tick		Comment
	My chant is good for playground games.	
	My chant has a repeating rhythm.	
	My chant has a rhyme pattern.	
	My chant is fun to say out loud.	

Traditional Tales

Outcome

A traditional tale, written as a group, plus mobile displays

Objectives

Word

10 [be taught] new words from their reading and shared experiences.

Sentence

1 to expect written text to make sense and to check for sense if it does not.

2 to use awareness of the grammar of a sentence to predict words during shared reading and when rereading familiar stories.

Text

2 to use a variety of cues when reading: knowledge of the story and its context, and awareness of how it should make sense grammatically.

5 to understand how storybook language works and to use some formal elements when retelling stories.

7 to use knowledge of familiar texts to re-enact or retell to others, recounting the main points in correct sequence.

12 through guided and independent writing, to experiment with writing and recognise how their own version matches and differs from conventional version.

13 to think about and discuss what they intend to write, ahead of writing it.

Early learning goals

- Extend vocabulary, exploring the meaning and sounds of new words.
- Explore and experiment with words, sounds and texts.
- Use phonic knowledge to write simple regular words and phonetically plausible attempts at more complex words.
- Use talk to organise, sequence and clarify thinking, ideas, feelings and events.
- Use language to recreate roles and experiences.
- Retell narratives in the correct sequence, drawing on language patterns of stories.

How you could plan this unit

Day 1	Day 2	Day 3	Day 4	Day 5
Shared reading Read several traditional tales. Make a list of key features: moral; elements of reality that pass on traditional culture; written in the past; human/animal characters; specific settings. Encourage class to ask older relatives for oral examples	**Talk for writing** Explore structure of stories (story sandwich, Resource Page B). Use story circles to recognise start, problem, events, resolution, end. Pass story hat around circle, each child adding to the story. Invite storyteller into school to tell traditional tales	**Shared reading** Read *The Magic Coin* (Resource Page A). Refer to story sandwich model and identify start, problem, events, resolution, end. Highlight key features from Day 1. Model story building on the board by arranging the parts of the story	**Talk for writing** *Starting Writing*	**Shared writing** *Story Problems*

Day 6	Day 7	Day 8	Day 9	Day 9 (cont.)
Reading and writing *Developing the Story*	**Shared writing** Story resolution. Discuss moral of tale: greedy farmer ends up with nothing. The children discuss what they would choose if granted one wish. Model how to compose the resolution. Independently, the children draw or write own wish	**Shared writing** *Story Endings*	**Display** Photocopy the completed story frames, one for each author. Laminate the master copy for each group and cut it into strips to hang down as a story mobile from a hoop or hanger. Hang the mobiles over a collection of	traditional tales and the plasticine coins displayed on the corrugated fields. The children make 'gold' coins to hang on the mobile and decorate the hanger on a 'gold' theme

Starting Writing

Objective

Together we will write the start of a traditional tale

You need: Resource Pages A–D; art materials.

Sentence-level starter

- Write the following sentence on the board for the class:

> He lived in a house.

- Explain that although it is a sentence (because it makes sense), it is a boring sentence.

- Challenge the children to make it more interesting by giving you ideas in answer to the questions:
  - *What sort of house is it?*
  - *What is the house made of?*
  - *What colour are the doors and windows?*

- Rewrite the sentence, using a selection of the children's responses.

Whole class work

- Reread the start of *The Magic Coin* (Resource Page A) with the class. Refer back to the story sandwich (Resource Page B) and remind your class that this is the top slice of bread.

- Discuss the key features of the start of a traditional tale:
  - It happened long ago.
  - It introduces the character, using 'here lived'.
  - It tells you where the story is set.
  - It gives some detail to help you imagine the setting.

- Model how you are going to use these key features to start to write your own traditional tale. Use Resource Page C as a prompt.

- Check with the class to see that you have included the key features.

- In pairs, the children discuss possible characters and settings, generating ideas.

Independent, pair or guided work

- In guided groups, work with the children to develop their initial ideas and orally compose a story start.

- Check with the group that they have made it a traditional story start.

- Discuss word choice, showing how to improve a simple sentence by adding detail.

- When the group is happy with the story start, scribe it on to the first section of the writing grid (Resource Page D), reading aloud as you write.

- The children not working in an adult-guided group can draw or paint their story setting.

Plenary

- ***What makes a good story start?*** Read story starts and ask the children to close their eyes and see if they can imagine the story setting.

- Challenge the children to tell you what helps them imagine the setting – identify that word choice is very important.

Story Problems

Objective

Together we will write a story problem, using traditional language

You need: Resource Pages A–D; children's story frames from the previous lesson; dressing-up clothes.

Word-level starter

- Investigate alliteration of the letter 'f' with your class. Try the tongue twister, 'Five fat funny flappy fish fell flop.'

- In pairs, the children try to work out the first sound they can hear. Identify that all the words start with an f sound.

- Draw a large fish on the board and challenge the children to vote yes (thumbs up) or no (thumbs down) for the words that might go inside the fish – only words that start with 'f' are allowed inside the fish. Say a selection of words, stressing the initial sound. Give the children time to repeat the word before voting.

fish	cat	face	finger	mouse
dog	fern	fiddle	field	fill

Whole class work

- Reread the second section of *The Magic Coin* (Resource Page A) with your class.

- Refer to the story sandwich (Resource Page B) and discuss how the story now introduces a problem, often represented by a character weakness.

- Discuss the use of alliteration in 'fern-filled fields' and reinforce the word-level work.

- Model how to write the story problem, using Resource Page C as a prompt.

- In pairs, the children think of problems that could be used in the group story.

Independent, pair or guided work

- As in the previous lesson, work with guided groups to scribe their version on to the writing frame (Resource Page D).

- When not working in a guided group, the children explore the story content through role play, acting out the farmer's dream of living in a grand house.

Plenary

- Recap alliteration by challenging the class to try some traditional tongue twisters:

> Round and round the ragged rock the ragged rascal ran.
>
> She sells seashells on the seashore.
>
> Peter Piper picked a peck of pickled pepper.

- *Can you hear and say the initial sound being used in each one?*

- Repeat the tongue twisters very slowly, then very fast for fun.

Developing the Story

Objective

We will develop our story by showing what happens next

You need: Resource Pages A–D; children's story frames from previous lessons; plasticine; gold foil.

Word-level starter

- Choose phonemes that your class is learning in phonics work. Ask the children to imagine a large volume control knob, which can turn to change the volume. Hold up a flashcard of one of your focus phonemes, and ask the class to whisper the sound that it makes. As you turn the volume control up, the class whisper gets louder and louder (but still a whisper). Turn the volume back down again and repeat with different phonemes.

Whole class work

- Reread the third section of *The Magic Coin* (Resource Page A) with the class.

- Highlight and discuss key features of the text:

  > 'Early one morning' — tells us when the story takes place.
  >
  > The farmer speaking — how does he speak?
  >
  > 'Suddenly' sentence — something important happens.

- Model your own version of the events on the board, using Resource Page C as a prompt.

- Read the new version with the class, pointing to the text word by word as you read it together. Concentrate on developing expression by stressing the word 'suddenly'.

Independent, pair or guided work

- As on previous days, work with guided groups to plan and scribe a group version of events.

- Guide the children to attempt the modelled features, by asking the questions:
  - *What time of day shall we make our events happen?*
  - *What shall we make him find?*
  - *What do you think he would say?*
  - *Let's think of a magical thing to happen in our 'suddenly' moment.*

- Write each group's events on the next section of their writing frame (Resource Page D).

- Independent groups use plasticine to roll coins to be covered in gold foil for the story display.

Plenary

- Refer back to the story sandwich (Resource Page B). *How far down the sandwich is our traditional tale now?*

- Revise the parts of the story sandwich. *Which part will come next?*

Story Endings

Objective

We will write a good ending for our traditional tale

You need: Resource Pages A, C and E; children's story frames from previous lessons; whiteboards; corrugated card; sponges; green and brown poster paint.

Word-level starter

- Use the phonemes that you are currently learning for this starter. Give out whiteboards and pens. Explain that this challenge is to see how well they can help each other to get a right answer. In pairs, as you say a phoneme, each child writes the letter(s) that represents it on their whiteboard and shows it to their partner. If they both have the same letter(s), they hold up their whiteboards. If their attempts differ, they discuss the difference with their partner and agree which one they think is right.

Whole class work

- Reread the end of *The Magic Coin* (Resource Page A) with your class.

- Discuss how traditional tales often have a 'moral' ending – they try to teach us a lesson.

- Refer back to a previous lesson, when your class investigated ways of adding detail to improve a sentence. Explain how the author has not just written 'in the earth' but 'in the rich brown earth'. **Which two describing words have been added to improve the sentence?**

- Model your version of the ending, using Resource Page C as a prompt. As you write, explain the choices that you are making as a writer.

Independent, pair or guided work

- In guided groups, the children work to orally compose a traditional tale ending.

- Scribe the story ending on the writing frame for each group.

- The children working independently recreate the colours and textures of the ploughed field in the story by sponge-painting corrugated card.

Plenary

- Read each group's story ending for the rest of the class. Discuss what makes them good story endings and extract the morals from the stories. Refer to Resource Page E.

Pupil copymaster

The Magic Coin

Long ago, in the days when the world was far younger than it is today, there lived an old farmer. He lived in a small, stone farmhouse with ivy creeping up the walls and in through the green-painted windows.

The farmer led a good working life, but he was never happy. Work as he might, he never could raise the living from his fern-filled fields that he felt he deserved. He dreamt of living in a grand house, with lace at the windows and candlesticks of silver to light his table.

Early one morning, as the farmer ploughed his fields, he spotted something glinting in the furrows of rich brown soil. Whatever could it be? The farmer bent down and scooped up the mysterious object.

"Well, stone the crows!" exclaimed the farmer, "'Tis a golden coin! But not one as I've ever seen the like of before ..."

Suddenly, as he rubbed the coin, to see the markings more clearly, a cloud of golden dust flew from his hand and circled the air around his head.

"What is your wish?" asked the gold. "Speak, and I will obey."

But the farmer just couldn't decide what he wanted the most, whispering to himself, "Oh, I want so much ... I wish I didn't have to choose!"

"Your wish is granted!" replied the coin, spinning from his hand and landing in a far corner of the field.

So the old farmer lived the rest of his life ploughing his fields, always watching, always hoping for another flash of gold in the rich brown earth. He knew that if he were ever given a wish again, he would not waste his chances by wanting too much.

But the magic coin was never seen again.

Pupil copymaster

A story sandwich

Story start

Who, what, where, when, why?

Something happens

Things are sorted out

Story end

(Exemplar material)

Modelled writing

The Magic Shell

Long ago, there lived a fisherman.

He lived on the seashore, in a rickety house made of driftwood washed up by the sea.

The fisherman was a lazy man. He sent his sons out to fish far from home and shouted at them when they did not bring home enough fish in the morning.

Late one evening, as he folded his nets, the fisherman spotted something caught in the ropes.

"My, a shiny shell of pearl!" he exclaimed, and rubbed the shell to see the colours more clearly.

Suddenly, the shell started to glow.

"What is your wish?" asked the shell.

"Oh, I wish you hadn't asked me that!" said the fisherman, "I just can't decide."

The shell jumped from his hands and landed with a splash in the sea.

So the fisherman lived out the rest of his life searching the yellow sandy shores for the magic shell, to make a wiser wish. But he never found that shell again.

(Pupil copymaster)

Writing frame

A traditional tale written by _____

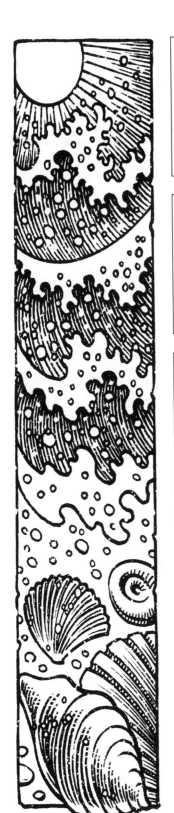

Story start

Story problem

Something happens

Resolution

Story ending

PHOTOCOPIABLE · PHOTOCOPIABLE

(Exemplar material)

Checklist for traditional tales

- Use traditional language

- Describe the characters

- Tell the reader details: Who? What? Where? When? How?

- Show the problem!

- Suddenly … something happens

- Solve the problem

- Use alliteration

- Give the ending a moral

Marking ladder

In Foundation Stage Reception, work is likely to be assessed orally with the child, at the point of writing. The features identified as a checklist can be used to provide a focus and any comments recorded as a marking ladder.

Name: _____

Tick		Comment
	I have used traditional language.	
	I have described the characters.	
	I have told the reader details: who, what, where, when, how?	
	I have shown the problem.	
	I used 'Suddenly' and something happened.	
	I solved the problem.	
	I used alliteration.	
	I gave the ending a moral.	

Instructions

Outcome

A set of instructions for planning a party

Objectives	**Word** **10** [be taught] new words from their reading and shared experiences. **11** to make collections of personal interest or significant words and words linked to particular topics. **Sentence** **1** to expect written text to make sense and to check for sense if it does not. **Text** **11** through shared writing: to understand that writing can be used for a range of purposes, e.g. to send messages, record, inform, tell stories. **13** to think about and discuss what they intend to write, ahead of writing it. **15** to use writing to communicate in a variety of ways.
Early learning goals	• Extend vocabulary, exploring the meaning and sounds of new words. • Explore and experiment with words, sounds and texts. • Use phonic knowledge to write simple regular words and phonetically plausible attempts at more complex words. • Interact with others, negotiating plans and activities and taking turns in conversation. • Use talk to organise, sequence and clarify thinking, ideas, feelings and events. • Use language to recreate roles and experiences.
Note	• This unit can be linked to Religious Education and have a 'celebrations' focus.

How you could plan this unit

Day 1	Day 1 (cont.)	Day 2	Day 3	Day 4
Shared experience Circle time – the children speak about their experiences of parties. Write on the board some of the key features. With response partners, the children make an oral list of things you need for a good party. The children	draw a picture of a party, with written commentary. Discuss how things need to be done in order	**Discussion for writing**	**Shared writing**	**Shared reading and writing** Use Resource Page C to compose own party menu. Note key features, information is in list format. Discuss features of a list. Model writing a menu. The children cut out pictures of food from magazines to decorate menus
		Planning a Party	*Writing an Invitation*	

Day 5	Day 6	Day 7	Day 8	
Shared and independent writing	**Shared experience and drama** Discuss games we like to play at parties. The children work in pairs to dramatise a favourite party game for others to guess. The children give instructions for how to play their chosen game	**Shared writing**	**Shared experience** Party! If appropriate, ask a parent to video the party, for use in a plenary discussion, or take photos that can then be used to illustrate the set of instructions	
Making a Shopping List		*Writing Instructions*		

49

Planning a Party

Objective

We will think about why you need instructions and how to organise them

You need: Resource Pages A and I; magnetic letters and board; whiteboards; teddy bear; sample invitations; large sheet of paper for checklist.

Word-level starter

- Write the word 'invitation' in large letters on the board.

- Use magnetic letters underneath, to recreate the word. Explain how when you look inside a big word, you can often see little words hiding. Use the magnetic letters to exemplify 'it' and 'tin'.

- Ask the children to work in pairs on whiteboards to see how many little words they can generate. You or your teaching assistant can guide some in a group.

Whole class work

- Refer back to the previous lesson, and the key features of a good party.

- *We need to explain to the teddy bear how to plan a great party because he doesn't know. He wants to invite his teddy friends. We need to give him a set of instructions to help him.* Review the list from the previous lesson and identify through discussion that: *First we need to decide on the time, date and place of the party to send out invitations*. You could use the song 'Teddy Bears' Picnic' to help the children think about what those bears would have needed on their invitations.

- Together, read the example invitation (Resource Page A) and other examples of invitations.

- Identify key features of an invitation and record as a class checklist (see Resource Page I for ideas).

- Together, plan the details of the class party, discussing purpose, date, time of day and which room in the school would be best.

- Read the checklist together, answering the points one by one.

Independent, pair or guided work

- Ask the children to draw a picture of the toy that they would like to invite and independently attempt to write the toy's name underneath.

Plenary

- Look at some examples of invitations. Using the class checklist, ask the children if they can identify all the elements on the invitation. *Are there any different ones? Are there any elements missing that are on the checklist?*

- Investigate the unusual letters that we often see at the bottom of invitations. *Does anyone know what R.S.V.P. means?* The children discuss with response partners.

- Explain that the initials stand for the French words for 'please reply' – *Repondez s'il vous plaît*.

- *Can we use those initials to think up any silly phrases?* 'Roses smell very pretty' or 'Rain starts vast puddles' or 'Rabbits see video pictures', and so on.

Writing an Invitation

Objective

We will write an invitation to a party for your favourite toy

You need: Resource Pages A and B; teddy bear; whiteboards.

Word-level starter

- Play 'Who am I?' The class sits in a circle with you. Using a whiteboard, start to write the name of one of the children, one letter at a time and pausing between letters. Choose children with phonically regular names to start with. The children look at the emerging name and try to guess who it is from the sounds they see appearing.

- As soon as a child recognises the name, they point to that child. You may need to consolidate the phonemes by sounding them out as you write them, depending on the stage of phonic progression within the group.

Whole class work

- Sit the teddy bear on your knee. The bear tells the class that he has heard a whisper about a party. *Is it true? Can all his friends come? Will you show him how to write a proper invitation so everyone can take one home for their toys?*

- Model writing an invitation using the example (Resource Page A) and the details from the previous lesson's party planning.

- Draw attention to the space for the child's name. In supported writing, the children practise writing their own name on individual whiteboards and show this to you or your teaching assistant. The children can keep their whiteboards to refer to later.

- Together, read the completed invitation.

Independent, pair or guided work

- The children use the blank invitation (Resource Page B) as a writing frame to write their own invitations for their favourite toy. Refer back to writing own names in shared writing and encourage the class to use their own name on the invitation.

Plenary

- Show a good example of a child's invitation and allow the child to explain how they solved problem aspects of composition, for example, *How did you know how to write this? Where did you find that word? Can you show us how you sounded that out?* Refer the children to the instructions on the class checklist.

Making a Shopping List

Objectives

We will write a shopping list for our party

You need: Resource Pages E and F; plastic play food or pictures of food.

Word-level starter

- Hold up items of plastic play food, or pictures of food, for example, bread, cake, fruit, jam.

- With the class, count together the number of phonemes that they can hear, holding up a finger for each sound. *Count the sounds you can hear, not the letters.*

  > j a m = 3   c a ke = 3   b r ea d = 4   f r ui t = 4

- Some children could try to count the sounds they can hear by themselves.

Whole class work

- Refer back to the previous lesson's scribed menu and read it together.

- With response partners, the children discuss what they think they would need to buy to make this meal.

- *Because we don't want to forget anything, we need to make a shopping list. Why is a list different from a story?* Discuss the key features of a list:

  > single food words
  >
  > no connectives
  >
  > organised vertically

- Model how to write a shopping list (see Resource Page E).

Independent, pair or guided work

- The children write their own shopping lists, using 'have a go' writing and blank templates (Resource Page F).

Plenary

- The children use their lists in role-play shopping, working in pairs or small groups to read out their lists to the shopkeeper. *Does your list use all the instructions on the class checklist?*

Writing Instructions

Objective

We will write a list of instructions for planning a party

You need: Resource Pages G–I; additional lists of instructions, for example, how to play a game; word processor.

Word-level starter

- Play 'I went to a party and I had …'. This helps to develop alliteration through a focus on the initial sounds in words.

- With your class sitting in a circle, each child adds an item beginning with the same sound to the list started by you. Start the first list with c, then try s and t. For example:

> I went to a party and I had cake … crisps … candy … cats … crocodiles …

- *How long can we make the list?*

Whole class work

- *Let's review all the things we have done so far to prepare for our party. So that we don't miss anything out, we need to write them down as a set of instructions.*

- *The order of instructions is important, if we did the shopping before we planned the menu we would find that we had bought the wrong food.*

- *The language of instructions is important too, we are telling people to do something, so we do need to sound quite bossy! Usually instructions start with a verb to support this, for example, 'take', 'make', 'write'.*

- *To help get the order right, we need to number the things that we need to do.*

- With response partners, the children see if they can work out the order for planning a party.

- Model how to write instructions (Resource Page G).

- Help your class to construct a checklist for writing instructions (see Resource Page I for ideas).

Independent, pair or guided work

- Working in pairs or small groups, the children write their own instructions for how to plan a party (using Resource Page H).

- Guided groups can use the computer to explore learning how to format their text using colour, interesting fonts, and so on.

Plenary

- Together, look at other examples of instructions, for example, recipes, games and so on, to see if the children can spot similar features:

> Are they organised in a list?
>
> Are they 'bossy'?
>
> Are they numbered in order?

- Consolidate the key text features of instruction writing, using the class checklist.

Invitation

Please come to my party!

Jessie is having a party.

Place: **At the swimming pool**

Date: **Saturday 29th November**

Time: **3pm – 6pm**

R.S.V.P.
5, School Road
Mytown
Telephone: 01349 257608

Pupil copymaster

My invitation

Please come to my party!

_____ is having a party.

Place: _____

Date: _____

Time: _____

R.S.V.P.

Classworks Literacy Year R © Julie Orrell, Nelson Thornes Ltd 2003

(**Pupil copymaster**)

Party menu

MENU

Cheese sandwiches

Crisps

Fruit

Jelly and ice cream

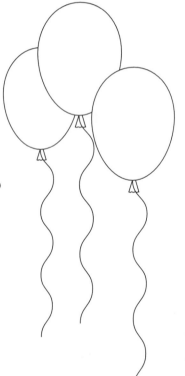

Birthday cake

Pupil copymaster

Party menu writing frame

MENU

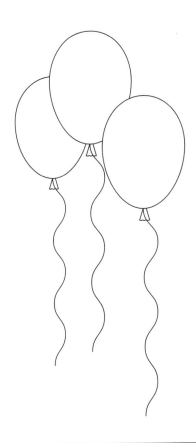

Pupil copymaster

Shopping list for the party

We need:

Balloons

Cake

Candles

Bread

Butter

Cheese

Fruit

Crisps

Jelly

Ice cream

Pupil copymaster

Shopping list writing frame

We need:

(Pupil copymaster)

Instructions – How to plan a party

1. Decide when and where your party will be.

2. Write your invitations.

3. Write a party menu.

4. Write a shopping list.

5. Plan your games.

6. Decorate the party room.

7. Prepare your party food.

8. Party!

Pupil copymaster

Party instructions writing frame

1.

2.

3.

4.

5.

6.

7.

8.

(Exemplar material)

Checklists for instructions

Example of a checklist for party instructions

- Think what you need to include before you write
- Write in a list
- Use numbers to show the order
- Use 'bossy' words
- Use a verb at the start of sentences

Example of a checklist for an invitation

An invitation needs to:

- Invite!
- Tell you the date
- Tell you the place
- Tell you the time
- Ask you to reply

Classworks Literacy Year R © Julie Orrell, Nelson Thornes Ltd 2003

Marking ladder

In Foundation Stage Reception, work is likely to be assessed orally with the child, at the point of writing. The features identified as a checklist can be used to provide a focus and any comments recorded as a marking ladder.

Name: _____

Tick		Comment
	I say it before I write it.	
	I think before I write.	
	I can write in a list.	
	I used numbers to show the order.	
	I used 'bossy' words.	
	I started with a verb.	

Classworks Literacy Year R © Julie Orrell, Nelson Thornes Ltd 2003

Stories with a Pattern 1

Outcome

A book using repetitive, patterned language, based on the structure of a shared text

Objectives

Word

2 knowledge of grapheme/phoneme correspondences through identifying and writing initial and final phonemes in CVC words.

4 to link sound and spelling patterns by using knowledge of rhyme to identify families of rhyming CVC words.

10 [be taught] new words from their reading and shared experiences.

11 to make collections of personal interest or significant words and words linked to particular topics.

Sentence

1 to expect written text to make sense and to check for sense if it does not.

4 to use a capital letter for the start of own name.

Text

9 to be aware of story structures.

13 to think about and discuss what they intend to write, ahead of writing it.

Early learning goals

- Extend vocabulary, exploring the meaning and sounds of new words.
- Explore and experiment with words, sounds and texts.
- Use phonic knowledge to write simple regular words and phonetically plausible attempts at more complex words.
- Use talk to organise, sequence and clarify thinking, ideas, feelings and events.
- Use language to recreate roles and experiences.

How you could plan this unit

Day 1	Day 2	Day 3	Day 4	Day 5
Shared reading Read *Six Dinner Sid* (Resource Page A). Focus on the form of the story – how it goes round in a circle. Identify and collect other story rounds. Tell stories in circles, each child contributing the next part of a class story	**Shared reading, drama, talk for writing** *Six Dinner Sid*	**Shared writing, supported writing** *Writing a Sentence (page 1 of book)*	**Shared writing, supported writing** Use sentence stem from Day 2 and vary the ending by the use of colour words. Model writing 'My cat is black and white.' Focus on colour words. The children write their sentence. This forms page 2 of their book	**Talk for writing** *Talking about Food*

Day 6	Day 7	Day 8	Day 9	
Shared writing *Writing about Food (page 3 of book)*	**Shared reading, writing** Where does Sid sleep? Vary the sentence stem to 'My cat likes to sleep in a ...' Model writing, then the children try independent but supported writing. This is page 4 of their book	**Shared writing** Focus back on story structure – the stories need to be circular. Revisit the first sentence: 'My cat is a ... cat.' Create the circle by remembering and writing the sentence. You could add 'very' for emphasis. This forms page 5	**Shared writing** Make a cover: title, illustration; assemble the pages in the right order to make a story round. Publish the cat story rounds and read to an audience (paired or group work)	

Six Dinner Sid

Objective

We will find good words for describing things

You need: Resource Pages A and B; a copy of *Six Dinner Sid* by Inga Moore (optional); a toy cat; magnetic letters; whiteboards; Blu-tack™.

Word-level starter

- Play 'Pass the rhyme' with the words 'cat' and 'Sid'. The children pass a toy cat around the circle, generating rhymes for the given word.

- Put the jumbled magnetic letters of 'cat' on a whiteboard. Sound out the phonemes c a t together, to model the correct order. Then verbalise for the class why the jumbled version is wrong.

- Challenge the children to unjumble the letters to spell 'cat' on their whiteboards.

Whole class work

- Read *Six Dinner Sid* to the class (Resource Page A).

- Model talking about the sort of cat you know, for example:

> I know a fierce/fluffy/friendly cat

- With response partners, the children tell each other about a cat they know.

- Use drama to encourage the children to act out the cat characters in the text: rough and tough, naughty, silly, smoochy, pouncing on a mouse, and so on.

- Then help the children to polish the drama to represent the text in mime. For example, when you point to an illustration in the book, can the children mime the cat's expression?

- Play 'Pass the cat'. Start off the circle with 'My cat is a greedy cat.' As the toy cat is passed around the circle, each child gives a describing word for a cat when the toy reaches them. Words can be repeated, but ensure that new and imaginative adjectives are singled out, explaining why they are effective. You could use human sentence cards (Resource Page B) and add different adjectives to vary the impact.

- Ask your class to vote on which version of the human sentence sounds best. ***Which cat would you most like to meet? Why?***

- Read out the chosen sentence: 'My cat is a … cat.' Ask your class to orally rehearse the chosen sentence, checking the number of words and conventions, for example starting with a capital letter and ending with a full-stop. The children can clap along with the words to check the number, and put their hands on their heads at the end to signify the end of the sentence and a full stop.

Plenary

- Using Blu-tack™, stick the human sentence cards on to the whiteboard, in the wrong order.

- In pairs, the children discuss with each other what the sentence *actually* says, and what it *should* say.

- One pair explains why the order is wrong and rearranges the words to make the original sentence.

- Repeat the exercise, with a different word order.

Writing a Sentence

Objective

We will write a sentence about the cat in our story

You need: Resource Pages A and B.

Word-level starter

- Ask the children to differentiate between sounds by making a 'meow' sound in a happy voice, a scary voice, a sleepy voice, a tough voice, a friendly voice, and so on.

- Repeat using phonemes <u>c</u> <u>a</u> <u>t</u> <u>s</u> <u>i</u> <u>d</u> (Progression in Phonics Step 2, Mood sounds).

Whole class work

- Reread Resource Page A to the class and discuss the meaning of the words used to describe Sid, focusing on adjectives. List these words on your whiteboard: 'rough', 'tough', 'silly', 'naughty', and so on. Highlight these as you read the text.

- Take suggestions for further additions to the list, recapping on adjectives generated in the previous lesson. This list forms an adjective word bank for supported writing.

- Model writing the sentence 'My cat is a ... cat.', explaining these points:
  - *Where do I start to write my sentence?*
  - *What do I want to say?*
  - Check the number of words – count and clap.
  - Use a capital letter at the start of a sentence for the word 'My'.
  - Leave a finger space between words.
  - Recall from yesterday the three phonemes in the word 'cat'.
  - Sound out the third word 'is'.
  - Identify the word 'a'.
  - Explain that the next word is an adjective chosen from yesterday. Check that understanding of describing words is clear.
  - Reread the sentence. *Does it make sense? We need the word 'cat' at the end again*. Ask for a volunteer to spell 'cat'.
  - Put a full stop to denote the end of the sentence.
  - Reread the sentence together, clapping out the words and putting hands on heads to represent the full stop.

Independent, pair or guided work

- The children repeat the shared sentence to their partners, 'My cat is a ... cat.'

- Challenge the pairs to change their sentence, by using a different adjective to describe their cat. Refer back to the word bank of adjectives.

- The children independently write their chosen sentence and draw a picture of their cat. This forms the first page of their individual stories.

Plenary

- Unjumble the word challenge. Extend the concept of jumbled CVC words, demonstrating by writing three versions of 'cat' on the board:

atc	cat	cta

- The children vote as to which they think is correct.

- This can be extended to unfamiliar words with three phonemes from the text, for example, 'Sid', 'vet', 'man'.

Talking about Food

Objective

We will choose a favourite food for Sid and label it

You need: Resource Page C; plastic toy food or pictures of food; plasticine, clay or junk for modelling.

Word-level starter

- Play 'Do you like this food?' (Resource Page C). The children use either yes/no response cards, or thumbs up/down to respond to CVC items of food written on cards:

fish	ham	jam	chips	bun	pop	rock

- Cover up a phoneme on each card (first, last, middle) and ask the children to tell you the missing phoneme by sounding out the word and identifying what is missing. Differentiate your questions to challenge at the child's phonic level.

Whole class work

- Pass an item of plastic food around the circle: the children respond with the sentence '**I like to eat [food item]**' or '**I don't like to eat [food item].**' You could then speed up the responses by passing more items so that several children are responding at once.

- With response partners, ask the children to tell their partner what their favourite meal would be.

- Draw a dinner for Sid and write the label 'fish and chips'.

- The children count the phonemes in f i sh and ch i p s.

Independent, pair or guided work

- In groups, make models of a delicious dinner for Sid, using clay, plasticine, junk and so on.

- Some children can independently write a label for each group, to tell Sid what the meal is, or you can write it for them.

Plenary

- Meals are set out with their correct labels. The children move around the tables, reading the signs to each other and discussing whether or not they would like to eat the meal too.

Writing about Food

Objectives

We will write a sentence, counting sounds and words carefully.
We will also learn to write the tricky word 'my'

You need: magnetic/card letters and board; whiteboards.

Word-level and sentence-level starter

- Model the skills of segmenting to spell, using the following phonemes as magnetic letters or cards:

| a | c | t | s | i | d | f | sh | ch | p |

The children count the sounds that they can hear in the following words, then use individual whiteboards to write the grapheme, to show the teacher which one is needed: 'cat', 'Sid', 'fish', 'chip', 'is', 'dish', 'sad'.

- Add the sight recognition word 'my' and investigate through sentence-level work how this bank of words can be rearranged to make a variety of sentences.

Whole class work

- Model the sentence '**My cat likes to eat fish and chips**.', explaining:
  - use of capital letter
  - word spacing
  - CVC segmenting of 'cat'
  - use of food label from previous lesson to help spell 'fish' and 'chips'
  - punctuation.

- Ask the children to read the sentence together, tracking word by word. The children can put hands on heads to denote the full stop at the end of the sentence.

- With response partners, the children orally rehearse which food they will use to end their sentence.

Independent, pair or guided work

- The children compose a sentence that describes what their cat likes to eat.

My cat likes to eat …

- Some children will need the support of a writing frame, for example:

My _____ likes to eat _____ and _____ .

Plenary

- Compile a class list of things our cat likes to eat, using the flip chart or whiteboard. Ask each child to add their chosen item to the list.

- You then explain the differences in purpose and organisation between the forms of sentence, list and label that have been exemplified.

(Exemplar material)

Six Dinner Sid

Sid lived at number one, Aristotle Street. He also lived at number two, number three, number four, number five and number six. Sid lived in six houses so that he could have six dinners. Each night he would slip out of number one, where he might have had chicken, into number two for fish … on to number three for lamb, mince at number four, fish again at number five rounding off at number six with beef and kidney stew.

Since no one talked to their neighbours in Aristotle Street, no one knew what Sid was up to. They each believed the cat they fed was theirs, and theirs alone.

But Sid had to work hard for his dinners. It wasn't easy being six people's pet. He had six different names to remember and six different ways to behave.

When he was Scaramouche, Sid put on swanky airs. As Bob he had a job. He was naughty as Satan and silly as Sally. As Sooty he smooched but as Schwartz he had to act rough and tough.

All this work sometimes wore Sid out. But he didn't care as long as he had his six dinners. And, besides, he liked being scratched in six different places and sleeping in six different beds.

In fact, life in Aristotle Street was just about perfect for Sid, until one cold damp day, he caught a nasty cough. The next thing he knew, he was being taken to see the vet. Poor Sid, he was taken not once … not twice … but six times! He went with six different people, in six different ways.

The vet said Sid's cough wasn't nearly as nasty as it sounded, but, to be on the safe side, he should have a spoonful of medicine. Of course, Sid didn't have just one spoonful of medicine. He had six!

Now, one black cat does look much like another, but nobody, not even a busy vet, could see the same cat six times without becoming suspicious. Sure enough, when he checked in his appointment book, the vet found six cats with a cough – all living in Aristotle Street!

So he rang the owners at once and, oh dear, Sid was found out! When they discovered what he had been up to, Sid's owners were furious. They said he had no business eating so many dinners. They said, in future, they would make sure he had only one dinner a day.

But Sid was a six-dinner-a-day cat. So he went to live at number one, Pythagoras Place. He also went to live at numbers two, three, four, five and six. Unlike Aristotle Street, the people who lived in Pythagoras Place talked to their neighbours. So, right from the start, everyone knew about Sid's six dinners. And, because everyone knew, nobody minded.

Inga Moore

(**Pupil copymaster**)

Human sentence cards

My	cat
is	a
_____	cat
	.

(**Pupil copymaster**)

Do you like this food?

jam	chips
fish	ham
pop	bun
rock	

Exemplar material

Checklist for stories with a pattern 1

- The story makes a round

- There is a list of adjectives to describe cats

- Say it before we write it

- Hear and write sounds in words

- Use a full stop at the end of a sentence

- Use capital letters at the start of a sentence and for names

- Write the tricky word 'my'

- Colour words

- Make the book cover exciting

- Use a title

Marking ladder

In Foundation Stage Reception, work is likely to be assessed orally with the child, at the point of writing. The features identified as a checklist can be used to provide a focus and any comments recorded as a marking ladder.

Name: _____

Tick		Comment
	Our story makes a round.	
	We used a list of adjectives to describe cats.	
	I say it before I write it.	
	I can hear and write sounds in words.	
	I used a full stop at the end of a sentence.	
	I used capital letters correctly.	
	I can write the tricky word 'my'.	
	I coloured words.	
	I made the cover exciting.	
	I used a title.	

Poems with Predictable Structures

Outcome

A poem using the repeating structure of a shared text; individual poems for a poetry puzzle display

Objectives

Word

1 to understand and be able to rhyme through: recognising, exploring and working with rhyming patterns; extending these patterns by analogy, generating new and invented words in speech and spelling.

4 to link sound and spelling patterns by using knowledge of rhyme to identify families of rhyming CVC words.

Sentence

4 to use a capital letter for the start of own name.

Text

10 to reread and recite stories and rhymes with predictable and repeated patterns and experiment with similar rhyming patterns.

12 through guided and independent writing, to write their own names.

13 to think about and discuss what they intend to write, ahead of writing it.

14 to use experience of stories, poems and simple recounts as a basis for independent writing, e.g. retelling, substitution, extension, and through shared composition with adults.

Early learning goals

- Explore and experiment with words, sounds and texts.
- Use phonic knowledge to write simple regular words and phonetically plausible attempts at more complex words.
- Begin to form simple sentences, sometimes using punctuation.
- Enjoy listening to and using spoken and written language, and readily turn to it in their play and learning.
- Listen with enjoyment and respond to rhymes and make up their own rhymes.

Note

- Before starting this unit, take photographs of your class.

How you could plan this unit

Day 1	Day 1 (cont.)	Day 2	Day 3	Day 4
Personal experience Take photos of your class for use later in the unit. The children walk in two circles: clockwise and anti-clockwise. Meeting another child, they shake hands and repeat, "My name is …" Scatter flashcards with the names of the class and	the children search for their own name. They practise writing own name	**Shared reading**	**Planning for writing, drama**	**Shared reading**
		Word Order	*Silly Names*	*Rhyming Pairs*

Day 5	Day 6
Modelling and writing	**Reading** Read the new verses of the poem in pairs. Glue each child's photo to the writing frame underneath their poem. Cover the photo with a 'lift the flap' cover and display the poems as a 'What is my name?' puzzle
Writing a Verse	

Word Order

Objective

We will find, read and write the repeating words in the poem

You need: Resource Pages A and B; magnetic letters; whiteboards; highlighter pen.

Word-level starter

- Using magnetic letters, demonstrate how to segment the word 'is' into two sounds i̲ and s̲, to spell it.

- Hide the two letters among other letters on the board, and ask for a volunteer to find them again. When a child finds the two letters, ask them to explain how they recognised them. Verbalise this for the class, for example, the 's' looks like a snake, s̲ is for snake.

- Using whiteboards, the children try to write the word 'is'. Demonstrate the formation of the letters on your board to support them.

Whole class work

- Read the poem *My name is ...* (Resource Page A) with your class, encouraging them to enjoy the humour of the text.

- Ask the children what they have noticed about the poem and scribe their observations.

- Focus on the repeating sentence stem 'My name is ...' and highlight where this occurs in the first line of the text.

- In pairs, the children discuss where they can see that same pattern of words in the poem. Using the highlighter pen, pairs of children are given the chance to show where they have spotted it by highlighting the shared text.

- Model how to write the sentence stem, pointing out:
  - the order of the words
  - the capital letter in 'My'
  - the two letters representing the two phonemes in the word 'is'.

- Rewrite the sentence stem, but in the wrong order and challenge your class to explain why each version is wrong.

Independent, pair or guided work

- On whiteboards, guide your group in attempting to write the sentence 'My name is ...' and their own name. Support their composition by referring back to the teaching points from the shared work and encouraging independent writing.

- Independently, the children put in order three words cut up from the sentence strip (Resource Page B). The children stick the words in the right order on to a piece of paper and complete the sentence with their own name.

Plenary

- Reread the poem with your class, encouraging them to sound the 'My name is' pattern as you read. The repeating pattern will be highlighted in colour from your earlier shared work, so follow the text with your finger as you read, giving a visual prompt.

Silly Names

Objective

We will plan silly sentences for our poem

You need: Resource Page A (one per child); strips of card; Blu-tack™; whiteboards (one per child).

Word-level starter

- Ask the children to write their name on individual whiteboards (support as needed).

- *How many words are there in your first name?* Are there any with two, for example, Mary Rose, Kelly Ann, John Paul? Model how you can show that the names are joined up by joining them with a little line – a piece of 'word string' to join them together.

- In pairs, the children work with their partner to write their own and their partner's names on a whiteboard, joining them up to invent a new two-word name.

- In turn, pairs of children read out their new joined-up names.

Whole class work

- Read the poem (Resource Page A) with your class, encouraging them to join in as you point to the words to demonstrate one-to-one correspondence.

- Focus on the silly names that the poet has used to make this into a nonsense poem.

- Point out that all of the names have:

> a capital letter at the start
>
> two or three words, joined by a hyphen
>
> really silly words – nonsense names.

- With response partners, the children talk about the silly names and invent some of their own. Remind them that they need two so that they have more than one word.

- Scribe the new silly names that the children invent on to strips of card, as planning for composition.

Independent, pair or guided work

- In guided reading, reread the poem and focus with your group on the repeating pattern, the capital letter at the start of names and the fact that all the names are either two or three words, connected with a hyphen.

- Independent groups illustrate their copy of the text by drawing pictures to represent the silly names that the poet has used.

Plenary

- Use Blu-tack™ to stick the silly name strips on to the board one at a time, reading each one to the class and asking them to check that the names fit the pattern. *Do they start with a capital letter? Do they have more than one word? Are they nonsense names?*

Rhyming Pairs

Objective

We will use new pairs of rhyming words to change a poem

You need: Resource Pages A and D; a toy.

Word-level starter

- Play 'Pass the rhyme'. Using the word 'me', pass a toy around the circle. As the toy gets to each child, they generate a word that rhymes with 'me', making a rhyme string.

- Ask an adult helper to scribe the words on the board as new ones are generated.

Whole class work

- Read the poem (Resource Page A) with the class, encouraging them to take over the reading where they are now confident to do so.

- Explore the rhyme pattern, identifying that it is the second and fourth lines that rhyme.

- *If we are going to write a new version of the last verse, our second line will have to rhyme with 'me' in 'And Riddle-me-ree, and ME'.*

- Cover up the word 'knee' in the final verse by sticking a slip of paper over the word. Show the class that you are doing this, to exemplify substitution.

- Challenge the children to remember as many words that rhymed with 'me' as possible from the word-level starter. Tick each word on the scribed list as it is remembered, and read the remaining words out together.

- Model how you can use these rhymes to help you make your new second line, for example:

> My name is Cake-for-tea
>
> My name is Buzzing-bee
>
> My name is Magic-key

- In pairs, the children explore this orally, using the 'me' rhymes (Resource Page D) to make up a silly name.

- Model recording your plan in picture form and explain to your class that this plan will help you remember your rhymes for tomorrow. For example, draw a cake sitting on a teapot.

Independent, pair or guided work

- Independently, each child draws a picture to plan the silly name rhyming with 'me' that they will use for their poem.

- Some children may be able to write the words under their picture.

Plenary

- Pairs of children act out their silly names for the rest of the class to guess!

Writing a Verse

Objective

We will write a new verse of the poem

You need: Resource Pages C (enlarged version and one per child) and E.

Word-level starter

- One by one, write the names of some of the children in your class on the board. Make deliberate errors by forgetting to use a capital letter at the start of some of the names.

- Challenge the class to spot what you have done wrong.

- Once this has been established, ask the class to vote on each of the names in turn, whether or not it is a proper name (has a capital letter). The children vote by showing thumbs up for yes, thumbs down for no.

Whole class work

- Model writing a new version of the poem on an enlarged version of the writing frame (Resource Page C).

> My name is Wobbly-jelly
> My name is Buzzing-bee
> My name is Crinkly-pasta-shapes
> And Riddle-me-ree, and ME.

As you work, identify to your class the following points:
- Capital letters at the start of lines of a poem and for names
- The repeating sentence stem 'My name is ...'
- The silly names substituted at the end of lines 1 and 3
- The rhyme at the end of line 2, using the planned words
- The hyphen to join the names together.

- Draw up these points for the class as a class checklist (see Resource Page E).

Independent, pair or guided work

- The children work in guided or independent groups to compose their new verse of the poem.

- Support this composition as appropriate through differentiated writing support: independent, writing frames, and so on.

Plenary

- Refer back to the checklist.

- The children read their own new verse, checking that it fits the checklist.

PHOTOCOPIABLE

Pupil copymaster

My name is …

My name is Sluggery-wuggery
My name is Worms-for-tea
My name is Swallow-the-table-leg
My name is Drink-the-sea.

My name is I-eat-saucepans
My name is I-like-snails
My name is Grand-piano-George
My name is I-ride-whales.

My name is Jump-the-chimney
My name is Bite-my-knee
My name is Jiggery-pokery
And Riddle-me-ree, and ME.

Pauline Clarke

Pupil copymaster

Sentence strips

My	name	is
My	name	is
My	name	is
My	name	is
My	name	is

Pupil copymaster

My name is …

by _____

My name is _____

My name is _____

My name is _____

And Riddle-me-ree, and ME.

PHOTOCOPIABLE · PHOTOCOPIABLE ·

Pupil copymaster

Words that rhyme with 'me'

pea	knee
tea	sea
bee	tree
key	three
free	me

PHOTOCOPIABLE · PHOTOCOPIABLE

(Exemplar material)

Checklist for poems with predictable structures

- Say it before we write it

- Use capital letters at the start of lines

- Repeat the sentence start – 'My name is ...'

- Use capital letters at the start of names

- Use rhyming words at the end of lines 2 and 4

- Choose silly names, with joined together words

Classworks Literacy Year R © Julie Orrell, Nelson Thornes Ltd 2003

Marking ladder

In Foundation Stage Reception, work is likely to be assessed orally with the child, at the point of writing. The features identified as a checklist can be used to provide a focus and any comments recorded as a marking ladder.

Name: _____

Tick		Comment
	I said it before I wrote it.	
	I used capital letters at the start of lines.	
	I repeated 'My name is …'.	
	I used capital letters at the start of names.	
	I used rhyming words in lines 2 and 4.	
	I wrote silly names, with joined together words.	

Classworks Literacy Year R © Julie Orrell, Nelson Thornes Ltd 2003

Signs and Lists

Outcome

Signs and lists for a class café role-play area

Objectives

Word

11 to make collections of personal interest or significant words and words linked to particular topics.

Text

1 through shared reading: to recognise printed and handwritten words in a variety of settings, e.g. labels, signs, notices; [to understand] that words can be written down to be read again for a wide range of purposes.

11 through shared writing: to understand that writing can be used for a range of purposes, e.g. to send messages, record, inform, tell stories.

12 through guided and independent writing: to experiment with writing and recognise how their own version matches and differs from conventional version.

13 to think about and discuss what they intend to write, ahead of writing it.

15 to use writing to communicate in a variety of ways.

Early learning goals

- Extend vocabulary, exploring the meaning and sounds of new words.
- Explore and experiment with words, sounds and texts.
- Use phonic knowledge to write simple regular words and phonetically plausible attempts at more complex words.
- Interact with others, negotiating plans and activities and taking turns in conversation.
- Use talk to organise, sequence and clarify thinking, ideas, feelings and events.
- Use language to recreate roles and experiences.

How you could plan this unit

Day 1	Day 2	Day 3	Day 4	Day 4 (cont.)
Shared experience Visit a café near school. Show how print is used to communicate information. Take photos of signs, labels and lists. Collect menus, printed napkins, food bags, mats. (Avoid deliberate mis-spellings eg 'lite bite'.) Make a cafe role-play area	**Shared reading** *Uses of Signs*	**Planning for writing** *Writing Signs*	**Shared writing** Use examples from Day 3. Is the information useful and clear? Discuss colour and size of 'fire exit' and 'first aid' signs. Show how to change font, colour and size on a computer. Choose class 'logo' together and identify one sign for each	group to produce in guided ICT time. In independent time, the children decorate paper hats with their name and logo, to wear when serving food

Day 5	Day 6	Day 7 onwards
Shared reading *Discussing Lists*	**Shared writing** *Writing a Menu*	**Role play** Model how to use signs to get information. Invite staff to your café, giving the class an opportunity to explain purpose of signs and use list-writing skills taking orders from menu. The children could make paper mats or napkins with logos

Uses of Signs

Objective

We will learn how signs give us information

You need: Resource Pages A, B (large and two per group) and F; clipboard and paper; large sheet of paper for checklist.

- Display the sentence cards (Resource Page A) as a human sentence, with a child holding each card.

- *Does the sign give us clear information? Does it give us concise information? Useful signs give us clear information in the fewest possible words. So we are going to play a human sentence game to try to make this into a useful sign.*

- Ask your class for suggestions as to which words are unnecessary.

- Gradually pare the sentence down to the two key words 'first aid'.

- Find the school first aid box or cupboard and see what the sign actually says.

Whole class work

- Read together the café sign cards (Resource Page B).

- In pairs, ask the children to answer the question, *Why do we need signs?*

- Discuss the different types of information that signs give us: warning, location, direction, specific information, persuasive. The information that they give is clear and concise.

- Identify that signs have particular features:
  - big, bold main statement
  - colour can be important
  - no unnecessary words
  - sometimes no words at all if the message can be conveyed in a symbol.

- Record the key features of signs as a specific checklist (see Resource Page F for ideas).

Independent, pair or guided work

- In guided groups, take your class on a 'sign hunt' around the school.

- Discuss how print is part of the environment.

- Discuss the signs that you find, modelling for the children strategies for reading the signs and discussing their purpose and organisation.

- Record the signs found on a clipboard.

- The children working independently use the café sign cards to play a visual discrimination game. Turn the pairs of signs over on the table and muddle them up. One by one, the children turn over two signs, trying to find a matching pair. When they do, they guess what the sign is telling us in order to 'win' the cards.

Plenary

- Hold up the sign cards one at a time as a quickfire flashcards game. The children call out what the sign 'says'.

87

Writing Signs

Objective

We will plan useful signs for our café

You need: Resource Page C; magnetic letters; whiteboards.

Word-level starter

- Using magnetic letters on the board, use the phonemes <u>b</u>, <u>c</u>, <u>g</u>, <u>h</u>, <u>n</u>, <u>p</u>, <u>sh</u> to investigate adding different initial sounds to the <u>ut</u> ending to make new words.

- Point out that the phoneme <u>sh</u> is a digraph – it has two letters but only one sound.

- List the new words to generate a rhyme string.

- Focus on the word 'shut' – count and sound out the three phonemes. Muddle the letters of 'shut' on the board, and challenge the children to unmuddle them on their whiteboards. Support by sounding out the three phonemes as the children write.

- Use the magnetic letters to segment and spell the correct order of letters in 'shut'.

Whole class work

- Use the recorded signs from your sign hunt in the previous lesson and work with your class to read the signs together.
    - *What sort of sign is this – warning or information?*
    - *What does the print say?*
    - *What does the symbol tell us?*
    - *Who do you think might read this sign?*

- In discussion, divide the signs into two groups: those which would be useful for the café and those which would not.

- In pairs, the children talk to each other about their experience of cafés, volunteering any other signs that they think we will need, for example, 'Toilet'.

- Model how to write the two signs 'Open' and 'Shut' on the board. As you write, refer to the word-level starter, counting the phonemes and demonstrating the process of transcribing sounds into letters. Verbalise the letter formation as you write each letter.

- On whiteboards, the children write the word 'shut' in supported composition. Before they write, sound out the three phonemes and support with modelled words.

- Each child checks their writing against your modelled word.

Independent, pair or guided work

- The children use the whiteboards to experiment with sign writing.

- Guide one group in using their phonic skills to attempt regular words and in making phonetically plausible attempts at harder words.

- Photocopy whiteboard examples as planning for the following lesson.

Plenary

- Read out these signs from the signs game (Resource Page C) one at a time, asking your class to vote (thumbs up/thumbs down) as to whether each one would be a useful sign in a café. Use this game to consolidate the planning for writing.

Discussing Lists

Objective

We will learn the features of lists

You need: Resource Pages D (or actual menu, one between two) and F; example of a book that contains a list.

 **Word-level starter**

- Play the 'I went to the cafe and I had ...' game. With your class sitting in a circle, start the game by completing the sentence stem with an item that starts with one of the sounds the children are learning in phonics work. The next child repeats the sentence and adds another item beginning with the same sound.

- See how far the class can make the order list go around the class before it gets too long to remember. Point out that you are making a spoken list.

Whole class work

- Read the sample menu (Resource Page D).

- In pairs, discuss what makes a menu format different from a story and add to the class checklist (see Resource Page F for ideas).

> A menu is presented as a list
>
> A menu is arranged vertically
>
> A menu has separate items that are not linked by conjunctions.

- Explain that now you have made the signs for your café, the next task is to make menus so that people coming to the café know what food you have. ***What would happen if a café didn't have a menu?*** Establish a purpose for the task.

- In pairs, the children discuss what they think would be good items for a café menu. Guide their discussion by reminding them that there should be a choice of starters, main courses, puddings and drinks so that the customer can have a whole meal.

- Take suggestions from your class and write ideas as a shared plan, recording them as a list. As you write, model the difference between spoken and written language by translating the suggestions into a common, concise format.

Independent, pair or guided work

- The children work in pairs reading the menus to each other and role playing customer and waiter. This may need to be acted out first by you and an assistant to guide the role play.

Plenary

- Read a story from the class book collection or library that contains a list (or read *Six Dinner Sid* from the earlier Stories with a Pattern unit).

- Challenge your class at the start of the plenary session to work out why you have chosen this particular story to read.

- After reading the story, the children work with response partners to discuss why you have chosen this book and to agree an answer.

- Review the key features of a list.

Writing a Menu

Objective

We will write a menu for our class café

You need: Resource Page E (enlarged and one per child); magazines with pictures of food; scissors and gluesticks; whiteboards.

Word-level starter

- Play the 'Dish of the day' game. Give your class individual whiteboards, and explain the game. You give the initial sound of a food that might be served in the restaurant. The children think about the sound and guess what food it might be that starts with the sound.

> s is for … sausage? sweets? spaghetti? sandwich? samosa?

- Each child then draws or writes the food they have thought of on their whiteboard.

- If the food that the child chooses begins with your given sound, then their food can be one of the dishes of the day.

Whole class work

- Using the planned list of ideas for a menu from the previous lesson, model how to write a menu.

- As you write, explain that you are:
  - using the class checklist to remind you how to write a list
  - organising your food list into starters, main courses, puddings and drinks, in other words sorting the content into sections
  - listing the names of the food and their prices, not writing sentences as you do in stories
  - using the sounds in words to help you know which letters to write.

- *Let's draw a picture by each meal to show the customer what the meal looks like. Restaurants often do this for the children, to help them decide what they want to eat. Pictures can add extra information.*

- After writing your modelled menu, check it with the class against the criteria on your checklist.

Independent, pair or guided work

- Differentiate your writing task to support the children as necessary in composing their own menus for the café. Encourage independent writers to 'have a go' at their own menus, using emergent writing, on the menu frame (Resource Page E). Work with a guided group of children with weaker transcriptional skills, modelling for them by scribing their contributions as a group menu.

- The children can illustrate their menus with drawings or cut-out pictures, and laminate the finished menus for use in the role-play area.

Plenary

- Together, look at the completed menus, reviewing how well they fit the checklist criteria. Celebrate the success!

- With your class, walk around the role-play area, reading the signs and displaying the menus.

Pupil copymaster

Sentence cards

If	you
need	First
Aid	then
you	can
look	in
this	box

Pupil copymaster

Café sign cards

Cafe	**First Aid** ✚
Special offer!	**Open**
Closed	**Toilets** 👉
Please pay here ⬇	*Mind the step*

(Pupil copymaster)

Signs game

Welcome	Please Pay Here ▼
Danger – falling rocks	*Menu*
Park and Ride	**Accident and Emergency Department**
Buy one, get one FREE!	*Special Offer!!*
Toilets	Fire Exit
No smoking	**First Aid** ✚

PHOTOCOPIABLE

Pupil copymaster

Café menu

MENU

£1

Ice cream

£1

Tomato soup

£2

Pie

£1.50

Chocolate cake

50p

Garlic bread

£3

Cheese salad

50p

Orange juice

£2

Egg, chips & beans

£3

Curry

25p

Milk

£3

Fish & chips

£2

Banana split

Pupil copymaster

Menu

PHOTOCOPIABLE PHOTOCOPIABLE

(Exemplar material)

Checklists for signs and lists

Example of a checklist for signs

- Signs give clear information

- Signs use the smallest number of words possible – or no words!

- Signs are to get our attention – to tell us information

Example of a checklist for lists ②

- Lists are written going down the page, not along the line

- Lists are to give you information or to help you remember things

- List menus are grouped in order (drinks, food, sweets)

Marking ladder

Marking ladder for signs

Name: _____

Tick		Comment
	I think before I write.	
	I know which signs you might find in a café.	
	I helped to make a sign using the computer.	
	My sign gave clear information.	
	I used size and colour to get my sign noticed.	
	I can read my sign.	

Marking ladder for lists

Name: _____

Tick		Comment
	I think before I write.	
	I write lists going down the page.	
	I don't use joining words.	
	My list gives information.	
	I used the sounds in words to help me spell.	
	I can read my list back.	
	My list makes sense.	

Classworks Literacy Year R © Julie Orrell, Nelson Thornes Ltd 2003

Nursery Rhymes

Outcome

A class nursery rhyme display, based on Humpty Dumpty

Objectives

Word

1 to understand and be able to rhyme through: recognising, exploring and working with rhyming patterns; extending these patterns by analogy, generating new and invented words in speech and spelling.

4 to link sound and spelling patterns by using knowledge of rhyme to identify families of rhyming CVC words.

10 [be taught] new words from their reading and shared experiences.

Sentence

1 to expect written text to make sense and to check for sense if it does not.

4 to use a capital letter for the start of own name.

Text

10 to reread and recite stories and rhymes with predictable and repeated patterns and experiment with similar rhyming patterns.

13 to think about and discuss what they intend to write, ahead of writing it.

14 to use experience of stories, poems and simple recounts as a basis for independent writing, e.g. retelling, substitution, extension, and through shared composition with adults.

Early learning goals

- Explore and experiment with words, sounds and texts.
- Use phonic knowledge to write simple regular words and phonetically plausible attempts at more complex words.
- Begin to form simple sentences, sometimes using punctuation.
- Hear and say initial and final sounds in words, and short vowel sounds within words.
- Enjoy listening to, and using, spoken and written language, and readily turn to it in play and learning.
- Listen with enjoyment and respond to rhymes and make up rhymes.

How you could plan this unit

Day 1	Day 2	Day 3	Day 4	Day 5
Talking, shared reading Nursery rhyme soap box. The children retell familiar nursery rhymes, and collect and display examples of nursery rhymes from library/book box/home. Guided reading focus. (You may wish to make a 'soap box' for pupils to stand on)	Shared reading, drama	Supported writing	Shared reading/supported writing	Shared writing
	Rhyming Pairs	*Word Order*	*Rhyme Strings*	*A New Rhyme*

Day 6	Day 6 (cont.)
Shared writing Model writing chosen version of the whole rhyme. The children use independent writing to compose their own rhyme. Differentiate writing support – independent/ partially in filled frame/scribed. This unit	could be extended to investigate the rhyme patterns of other nursery rhymes

Rhyming Pairs

Objectives

We will read *Humpty Dumpty* and listen for pairs of words that rhyme. We will also look for rhymes in other nursery rhymes

You need: Resource Pages A and E; a toy; a set of phoneme cards; whiteboards; 26 cereal boxes and paint; large sheet of paper for checklist

Word-level starter

- Use 'Pass the rhyme' game with the words 'wall' and 'men'. The children pass a toy around the circle, generating rhymes for the given word (Pebble game, Progression in Phonics Step 2).

- Use the word 'sat' to investigate rhyme generation by changing the first phoneme. Using phoneme cards, put <u>a</u> and <u>t</u> on the board. Give each child a phoneme card and sound out the resulting words as each child adds their card as initial sound, for example <u>c</u> <u>a</u> <u>t</u>, <u>b</u> <u>a</u> <u>t</u>.

- List the resulting words on the board to exemplify a rhyme string.

Whole class work

- Write the poem *Humpty Dumpty* on the board, then read or sing it to your class. (If the children know it, they can join in.)

- Point out the structure of four lines, each pair ending in a rhyme.

- Recite the rhyme again, this time omitting the last word in each line, and ask the children to supply the correct rhyme.

- Ask a volunteer to circle each capital letter on the board. With response partners, the children ask 'Why are these letters capitals?' Take suggestions, for example, 'Capital letters are at the start of sentences and for the first letter of a name.'

- Ask the children to write their own names on individual whiteboards using a capital letter at the start. These can be shared with you, your teaching assistant or the children's response partners.

- Encourage the children to display their understanding of the nursery rhyme with their response partners by asking, **Who is Humpty Dumpty? What do you know about eggs? What might happen if an egg fell off a wall? How could you try to put a broken egg back together again?**

Independent, pair or guided work

- In small groups, act out the rhyme with the characters: Humpty Dumpty, the king's horses and the king's men.

- Working individually or in pairs, ask the children to paint cereal boxes to resemble bricks on a wall (you need 26). When the boxes are dry, ask the children to glue one word from the rhyme on to each box (Resource Page A).

Plenary

- *Which other nursery rhymes can we think of that have rhymes at the end of the lines?* Use this to begin your class checklist (see Resource Page E for ideas).

Word Order

(Objective)

We will learn how the order of words changes the meaning of a sentence

You need: Resource Page B (one per child); whiteboards; painted word 'bricks' from previous lesson; coloured pencils or crayons.

Word-level starter

- Play 'Humpty Dumpty says, "Show me the sound."' Ask the children to use whiteboards to write graphemes, in order, in response to these spoken phonemes: s a l h d o w. The children can share with response partners, you or your teaching assistant.

Whole class work 1

- Together, the children recite the rhyme, using hand actions.

- The children make suggestions and work together to order the cereal boxes for the first line of the poem.

- Explore what happens when the order of the words is changed. ***Does it make sense?*** Discuss how when we read and write, the order of the words is important – changing the order changes the meaning. Ask the children: ***Why is it important to put a space between words?***

Whole class work 2

- Using a large space (hall or playground) the children choose a word box and read it to their response partner. (The children may need to share a box.)

- Together, the class recites the poem word by word, while the children order themselves into a human rhyme.

- When you have completed the rhyme, ask each child to read out their word in order, to make the rhyme.

- Ask the class to work out where the human rhyme needs to break to make the four lines of the poem. The class breaks up into four lines. If a child is at the start of a line, ask them to put their hands in the air to represent a capital letter. If they are at the end of a line, they sit down to represent a pause, comma or full stop.

Independent, pair or guided work

- Give each child a paper copy of the rhyme (Resource Page B) and ask them to annotate it. Some children may prefer to work in pairs.
  - *Colour the capital letters red.*
  - *Colour the rhyming words blue.*
  - *Draw a circle around each pair of rhyming words.*
  - *Colour the full stops green.*
  - *Draw a yellow line under any words that you can read to your partner.*

Plenary

- Using their coloured rhymes, revise these different reading strategies: phonic, sight recognition, context, grammar.

- Ask the children to read their yellow words to their partners, saying what the word is and explaining how they know what it is. Encourage the children to mime their word.

- Ask the class what they can add to their checklist.

Rhyme Strings

Objective

We will find and make pairs of rhyming words

You need: Resource Page C; a ball of string or wool; tape recorder.

Word-level starter

- Play 'Humpty Dumpty says: "Make me a rhyme string."' A ball of string is passed around the circle of children, unravelling as it goes. As each child gets the ball, they generate a rhyming word to add to the rhyme string. Rhyme starters: 'cat', 'dog', 'hen', 'mop', 'man', 'hat', 'jug', 'rock'.

Whole class work

- Model writing the first two lines of *Humpty Dumpty*, leaving out the two rhyming words at the end.

> Humpty Dumpty sat on a _____
>
> Humpty Dumpty had a great _____

- Ask your class for suggestions of new pairs of rhyming words. This will assess their level of awareness. Some children may be able to do this independently.

Independent, pair or guided work

- The children unable to generate rhyming pairs work in groups to play the 'Find a rhyming pair' game. Cut up the photocopied pairs of rhymes (Resource Page C) and turn them face down on the table. The children take turns to turn over two cards, to see if they have found a rhyme. At the end of the game, the group reads the rhyme pairs out aloud.

- The children able to generate rhyme pairs orally use a tape recorder and recite their new versions of the rhyme, for example:

> Humpty Dumpty sat on a bed,
> Humpty Dumpty had a great head

Plenary

- As a class, listen to the tape-recorded rhymes. If the children think it is a rhyme, they vote 'thumbs up'; if they don't think it is a rhyme they vote 'thumbs down'.

- If there are any unsuccessful rhymes, explain why the rhyme doesn't work and ask the class to suggest alternative rhymes.

A New Rhyme

Objectives

We will make new rhyming pairs for a nursery rhyme

You need: Resource Page D; whiteboards (one each); magnetic letters or cards; Post-it™ notes.

Word-level starter

- Model the skills of segmenting words in order to spell them, using the following phonemes: <u>a</u> <u>c</u> <u>t</u> <u>h</u> <u>d</u> <u>o</u> <u>g</u> <u>l</u>.

- Ask the children to count the sounds that they can hear, and write the graphemes on individual whiteboards for the words: 'hat', 'cat', 'dog', 'log'.

Whole class work

- Model writing a new version of the first two lines of the rhyme:

> Humpty Dumpty sat on a hat,
>
> Humpty Dumpty had a great cat.

- Explain why you are using capital letters, word spacing, CVC segmenting of 'cat' and 'hat', rhyme and punctuation.

- Ask the children to read the lines together, tracking word by word. The children put their hands on their heads to denote the full stop at the end of the second line.

- *Tell your response partner what you are going to write for your new rhyme. Response partners check that the words rhyme.*

Independent, pair or guided work

- Using photocopied writing frames (Resource Page D) on laminated or card strips, the children independently write pairs of rhyming words on Post-it™ notes to complete the lines. You can then use the Post-it™ notes and overlap them to make a selection of rhymes at the end of the lines, that is, individual 'lift the flap' rhyme cards.

Plenary

- Read the sentence strips, moving around the Post-it™ notes, so that the class can play 'Is it a rhyme?'

PHOTOCOPIABLE · PHOTOCOPIABLE

(**Pupil copymaster**)

Humpty Dumpty **word cards**

Humpty	Dumpty	sat
on	a	wall
Humpty	Dumpty	had
a	great	fall
All	the	king's
horses	and	all
the	king's	men
couldn't	put	Humpty
together	again	

Pupil copymaster

Humpty Dumpty

Humpty Dumpty sat on a wall,

Humpty Dumpty had a great fall.

All the king's horses

and all the king's men,

couldn't put Humpty together again.

Classworks Literacy Year R © Julie Orrell, Nelson Thornes Ltd 2003

PHOTOCOPIABLE · PHOTOCOPIABLE

(**Pupil copymaster**)

Rhyme pairs

wall	fall
mop	shop
dog	log
man	pan
hat	cat
jug	rug
rock	sock

PHOTOCOPIABLE · PHOTOCOPIABLE

(**Pupil copymaster**)

A new rhyme

Humpty Dumpty sat on a _____

Humpty Dumpty had a great _____

PHOTOCOPIABLE · PHOTOCOPIABLE

(Exemplar material)

Checklist for nursery rhymes

- Say it before we write it
- Use capital letters at the start of lines and for names
- Nursery rhymes have rhythms
- Nursery rhymes are meant to be spoken
- Use rhyming words at the end of lines

Marking ladder

In Foundation Stage Reception, work is likely to be assessed orally with the child, at the point of writing. The features identified as a checklist can be used to provide a focus and any comments recorded as a marking ladder.

Name: _____

Tick		Comment
	I say it before I write it.	
	I can hear and write sounds in words.	
	I used a full stop at the end of a sentence.	
	I used capital letters correctly.	
	I always put spaces between words.	
	I used rhyming words at the end of lines.	
	I can generate a rhyme string.	
	I can read my new nursery rhyme.	

Non-fiction: Recount

Outcome

A recount of a visit

Objectives	**Sentence**
	1 to expect written text to make sense and to check for sense if it does not.
	Text
	11 through shared writing, to understand that writing can be used for a range of purposes, e.g. to send messages, record, inform, tell stories.
	13 to think about and discuss what they intend to write, ahead of writing it.
	15 to use writing to communicate in a variety of ways.

Early learning goals

- Sustain attentive listening, responding to what they have heard by relevant comments, questions or actions.
- Use phonic knowledge to write simple regular words and phonetically plausible attempts at more complex words.
- Interact with others, negotiating plans and activities and taking turns in conversation.
- Use talk to organise, sequence and clarify thinking, ideas, feelings and events.
- Show an understanding of how information can be found in non-fiction texts to answer questions about where, who, why and how.
- Use language to recreate roles and experiences.

Notes

- This unit will support a cross-curricular theme, exemplified here by a visit to the Post Office. It could be repeated each term, with a different focus.

How you could plan this unit

Day 1	Day 2	Day 3	Day 4	Day 5
Shared experience Class visit, linked to curriculum focus. Take photographs of the main events of the visit, to sequence later. Collect brochures, signs, leaflets, posters, and so on to create a role-play area	**Shared reading** Read the two recounts (Resource Page A) with the class. What do they tell us? Which is better? Identify the following: key information – when, who, where, what, why; time order of sentences; detail to make it interesting	**Shared writing** *Planning*	**Shared writing** *Answering 'W' Questions*	**Shared writing** Reread second sentence from text 2, Resource Page A. Identify which questions are answered. Identify connective 'first' that tells us the order things happened. Model your own second sentence. Using the planning grid, the children

Day 5 (cont.)	Day 6	Day 6 (cont.)	Day 7	Day 8
write their second sentence on a sentence strip	**Shared writing** Reread the third sentence from text 2, Resource Page A. What is the author telling us? Can the children spot the time connective 'later'? Model your own third sentence. The children write their third sentence strip with aid of	planning grid using the word 'later'	**Shared reading** *Ordering Events*	**Shared writing** *Ordering Sentences*

110

Planning

Objectives

We will make a plan for writing our recount

You need: Resource Pages A–D; several objects that start with different sounds, for example, doll, brick, marble, crayon; tape recorder.

Word-level starter

- Play 'What is my first sound?' One at a time, hold up a collection of objects that start with different sounds, for example, doll, brick, marble, crayon, and so on.

- The children work in pairs to agree between them which sound the object begins with, by saying the word and stressing the first sound. Repeat. The second time, they make the sound with their partner as you hold up the object.

Whole class work

- Explain that good writers always think about what they want to say before they write. ***We are going to plan our recount to make sure that it tells the reader lots of information.***

- Give the class a real purpose for making their recount really good, perhaps to present to another class, or in assembly.

- Refer to the two examples from the previous lesson (Resource Page A), reinforcing that a good recount answers questions.

- Use the five question prompt cards (Resource Page B) to play a quick-fire recount game. Recalling the details of the class visit, hold up one card at a time and ask the children to call out an answer. You may need to repeat some question prompts if the children are not secure with their answers.

- Model how to record this information on an enlarged version of the blank writing frame (Resource Page C), using the modelled frame as a prompt (Resource Page D). This will act as a shared planning sheet for the class.

Independent, pair or guided work

- Working in pairs or in guided groups, play a game to develop questions and answers about the visit. Tape record a set of questions and play the tape question by question, stopping the tape to allow time for pairs to ask and reply to each other.

- Working with a response partner, the children ask and reply to the following questions:

> When did we go on our visit? ● When did we get back to school? ● Where did we go?
>
> Where did we have our lunch? ● Who went on our visit? ● Who looked after us?
>
> Who showed us around? ● What did we see? ● What did you like best?
>
> Why did we go on our visit? ● Why did we have to go on a bus?

Plenary

- Question the answers! Reread the shared plan, covering up the questions at the start of the rows. Challenge your class to guess the question from the answer on the plan.

111

Answering 'W' Questions

Objective

We will write a sentence telling when and where we went

You need: Resource Pages A–C.

Word-level and sentence-level starter

- Play 'Funny full stops'. Write on the board:

> A full stop finishes the sentence.

Read the sentence together, pointing to the words as you read them and putting hands on heads to signify the full stop at the end of the sentence.

- Using a red marker, put the full stop in the wrong place, then read the sentence again together. Stop reading at the full stop and put hands on heads. ***Does it make sense?*** Reinforce the concept that a sentence is a unit of meaning – it has to make sense.

- Repeat the game, with the full stop in various positions.

Whole class work

- Reread the first sentence of the second recount text (Resource Page A). Identify what it is telling the reader. Underline the three phrases:

> <u>On Saturday</u>   <u>to the toyshop</u>   <u>with Mum</u>

- Using the question prompt cards (Resource Page B) discuss which questions are being answered.

- Model your own first sentence for the class, for example:

> Last week Class 1 went to the Post Office on a bus.

Independent, pair or guided work

- The children use the writing frame (Resource Page C) to support them in writing their own first sentence. Differentiate the support by composing orally with groups who have lower transcriptional skills and guiding their writing by scribing their sentence for them. Photocopy the sentence for each member of the group.

Plenary

- Choose one child's sentence and encourage them to explain how they solved problems of composition, for example, ***How did you know how to write this? Where did you find that word? Can you show us how you sounded that out?***

Ordering Events

Objective

We will put the events for our recount in order

You need: Resource Page A; magnetic letters; books from the classroom collection; photos of your trip plus photocopies of three key photos (for each child); whiteboards; scissors; Blu-tack™; large sheet of paper for class list.

Word-level starter

- Using magnetic letters, make the word 'and' on the board.

- Sound out the three phonemes <u>a</u> <u>n</u> <u>d</u>, counting with your fingers as you sound them out.

- Muddle the letters, and sound out the resulting combinations – challenge your class to respond. *Give a thumbs up if it is the real word, thumbs down if it is a muddled up word.*

- Using whiteboards and working with a partner, encourage your class to have a go at writing the three sounds in 'and'.

Whole class work

- Write for your class the word 'and' in the middle of the board.

- Use a range of stories from the class book box to collect alternative words that move the story on and give it structure, for example, 'then', 'later', 'that afternoon'. Write these as a word bank of connectives on the board.

- In pairs, the children try to find the connectives in their copy of the second recount text (Resource Page A). *Underline the words that you find.*

- Using the photographs that you took on your visit, discuss the order in which events happened. Use Blu-tack™ to stick these in the right order on the board, modelling the words 'first' and 'later' between the photos.

Independent, pair or guided work

- Working in pairs, or in a small guided group, the children discuss with each other the order of the copied photos and arrange them on a sheet of paper.

- Challenge higher achieving children in your class to try to add a word to show the order.

Plenary

- Make a classroom list or display board of connectives that authors use, adding to it when you find new ones in class story time.

Ordering Sentences

Objective

We will order our own writing

You need: Resource Page E; sack or bin bag; phoneme cards; children's sentence strips from previous lessons; gluesticks; crayons or photos.

Word-level starter

- Play 'Inside the magic sack ...' Use a black bin bag or sack and pull out a card showing a letter sound, reflecting the phonemes you are teaching in phonics. Ask your class to make the sound on the card.

- Ask the children to talk with their response partners and think of things that begin with that sound.

- *Inside the magic sack there are lots of things that begin with that sound, but they are all invisible.*

- Challenge the children to come out in pairs and pull an invisible object from the magic sack that begins with the focus sound.

Whole class work

- Demonstrate to your class how you are going to cut up your model text into three strips (Resource Page E).

- Model how you can muddle them but use the words 'first' and 'later' to help put them back in order.

- Read the reassembled text together, encouraging your class to join in with you. Point at each word as you say it to show your class how the written words match the spoken ones.

Independent, pair or guided work

- In pairs (guided where needed), the children read their own three sentence strips to each other.

- Independently or in a guided group, the children work to assemble their three sentences into a recount.

- The sentence strips can then be stuck down and illustrated with drawings or photographs.

- The completed recounts could be given a Speaking and Listening focus through presentation to another class or in an assembly.

- Consider using the shared text or an example of a child's work as a text for guided reading to reinforce the learning.

Plenary

- Consolidate the key text features of recount writing by recording a class checklist (see Resource Page F for ideas). Encourage the children to come up with the things that they have learnt for the checklist. Use it to support recount writing on future occasions.

Pupil copymaster

Recount texts

1

I went to the shop and I bought a toy and I had a drink.

2

On Saturday I went to the toyshop with Mum. First we had a drink of orange because it was really hot. Later I met my friend Sara and she came home to play.

PHOTOCOPIABLE · PHOTOCOPIABLE

Exemplar material

Question prompt cards

When?
Where?
Who?
What?
Why?

Pupil copymaster

Planning frame for recount of our visit to the Post Office

When?	
Where?	
Who?	
What?	
Why?	

My sentence

_____

_____

Pupil copymaster

Plan for recount of our visit to the Post Office

When?	last week
Where?	to the Post Office
Who?	Class 1
What?	we saw the letters
Why?	to learn about sending letters

Useful words

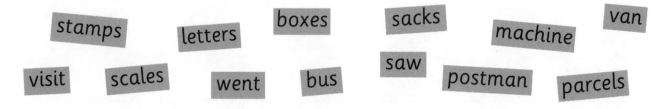

stamps letters boxes sacks van machine

visit scales went bus saw postman parcels

PHOTOCOPIABLE PHOTOCOPIABLE

Pupil copymaster

Modelled writing

Last week Class 1 went to the Post Office on a bus.

First we all looked at the letters.

Later we sat in Postman Pat's red van.

PHOTOCOPIABLE · PHOTOCOPIABLE

(Exemplar material)

Checklist for recounts

- Plan before you write

- Tell the reader:
  - When?
  - Who?
  - Where?
  - What?
  - Why?

- Put your sentences in the right order

- Use helpful words to show the order

- Use full stops

- Give lots of detail to make it interesting!

Classworks Literacy Year R © Julie Orrell, Nelson Thornes Ltd 2003

Marking ladder

In Foundation Stage Reception, work is likely to be assessed orally with the child, at the point of writing. The features identified as a checklist can be used to provide a focus and any comments recorded as a marking ladder.

Name: _____

Tick		Comment
	I planned my writing.	
	I answered ____ 'w' questions.	
	My sentences are in the right order.	
	I used helpful words to order my sentences.	
	I used full stops correctly.	
	I can read my recount back.	

Stories with a Pattern 2

Outcome

ICT sentences and labels using rhyme

Objectives

Word

2 [be taught] knowledge of grapheme/phoneme correspondences through identifying and writing initial and final phonemes in CVC words.

4 to link sound and spelling patterns by using knowledge of rhyme to identify families of rhyming CVC words.

10 [be taught] new words from their reading and shared experiences.

11 to make collections of personal interest or significant words and words linked to particular topics.

Sentence

1 to expect written text to make sense and to check for sense if it does not.

4 to use a capital letter for the start of own name.

Text

9 to be aware of story structures.

13 to think about and discuss what they intend to write, ahead of writing it.

Early learning goals

- Explore and experiment with words, sounds and texts.
- Hear and say initial and final sounds in words, and short vowel sounds within words.
- Write their own names.
- Use phonic knowledge to write simple regular words and phonetically plausible attempts at more complex words.
- Make up own stories, songs, rhymes and poems.
- Interact with others, negotiating plans and activities and taking turns in conversation.
- Use language to recreate roles and experiences.

How you could plan this unit

Day 1	Day 2	Day 2 (cont.)	Day 3	Day 4
Shared reading	**Talk for writing** The children make a circle. Pass a jar of jam around the circle, with request and response 'Pass the jam, Jim', 'Thanks a lot, Jim.' Repeat with other play food, supplying name rhyme, e.g. cheese/Louise. In role play,	the children set up a party table using the same pattern	**Planning for writing**	**Shared writing**
Writing Our Names			*Planning Rhymes*	*Writing a Sentence*

Day 5	Day 6	Day 6 (cont.)
Shared writing	**Display** Create an interactive literacy display of party food pictures. The children draw a picture of themselves. Display the faces around the table, with the children's speech captions from previous lesson. The	children stick food labels on to the display
Writing Food Words		

Writing Our Names

Objective

We will write our own names

You need: Resource Page A; large plastic hoop; alphabet cards; card for making name cards; whiteboards; large sheet of paper; sticky labels (one per child).

Word-level starter

- The children sit in a circle. Pass a name around the circle in the manner of Chinese Whispers, whispering it to the first child and challenging the class to get the name around the circle and back to you again.

- Play 'My name begins with ...' The children sit in a circle, with a hoop in the centre. One by one, hold up the letters of the alphabet. The children jump into the hoop when they see the letter their name begins with. Some children may need name cards for reference.

- Using individual whiteboards, the children attempt the first letter in their name.

Whole class work

- Read *Pass the jam, Jim* (Resource Page A) with your class.

- Discuss the role of names within the story, noting how they all start with a capital letter.

- Make a shared list on a big sheet of paper of all the names that you find in the story, to act as a word bank in later sessions.

Independent, pair or guided work

- The children who are able to write their names independently add them to the name chart. Challenge these children to look for more examples of names in the classroom book collection and add them to the list.

- Guide those unable to write their name, using whiteboards to teach them the formation and sequence of letters.

Plenary

- Give the children a sticky label and brightly coloured felt pens for them to design a name badge to wear.

- Remind the class that names start with a capital letter.

Planning Rhymes

Objective

We will plan a rhyme for our writing

You need: Resource Pages A and B; a picture of a jar of jam; magnetic letters; Blu-tack™; slips of paper.

Word-level starter

- Play 'Pass the rhyme' with the word 'jam'. The children pass a picture of a jar of jam around the circle, generating rhymes for 'jam'.

- Put the magnetic letters 'j' 'a' and 'm' on your whiteboard. Sound out the assembled phonemes of j a m together, to demonstrate segmenting to spell.

- Change the first magnetic letter of 'jam' to make new words 'sam' and 'pam'. Sound out the phonemes one at a time.

Whole class work

- Read *Pass the jam, Jim* (Resource Page A) to the class again and list the pairs of rhymes on the board as you read. **Work with your partner to agree which are the rhymes for 'Dot', 'Lee' and 'Fred'.**

- *Can we make some new rhymes that could have been used in the story? Let's look at the word bank of names we made before. Can we find any rhymes in our class?*

- Using the rhyming pair cards (Resource Page B), use Blu-tack™ to stick one of each pair of words on your board. Model for your class how you are going to sound out the word and change the first sound to make a new rhyming word.

- Discuss the first letter in all the names and reinforce that names start with capitals.

- Model how you are going to choose a pair of words: one food and one name. Check that they rhyme by sounding them out, and then use Blu-tack™ to stick them to your board as a writing plan.

Independent, pair or guided work

- Provide some cut up rhyming pair cards (Resource Page B) and some blank slips of paper for your guided group.

- The children work on choosing a name and a rhyming food from the rhyming pair cards. Some children may be able to generate their own.

- With response partners, the children check whether their words rhyme.

- The children write their names on the back of their papers and save as a writing plan.

Plenary

- Challenge your class to decide whether or not the following pairs of words rhyme. The children respond with thumbs up if it is a rhyme and thumbs down if it is not.

mouse / house	pig / pen
ten / hen	horse / course
cat / horse	fish / dish
dog / frog	pig / wig
rat / hat	dog / man

Writing a Sentence

Objective

We will write a sentence on the computer using our plans

You need: Resource Pages A and C; infant word-processing programme, with a saved sentence stem 'Pass the ...', or interactive whiteboard.

- Demonstrate how you can use the same sound at the start of words to make an alliterative name, for example: 'happy Harriet', 'sad Sara', 'daring Daniel'.

- Choose names one by one and ask your class in pairs to decide on an alliterative describing word for that name.

Whole class work

- Model how to compose your sentence stem 'Pass the ...' on the computer, or using an interactive whiteboard.

> Use a large point size and a child-friendly font.
>
> Leave a space between words using the space bar.
>
> Hold down the shift key for a capital letter, as all names start with a capital letter.
>
> Use a full stop to show that your sentence is complete.

- Use the pair of words that you planned in the previous lesson, and model how you are going to add them to the stem to make a sentence, for example:

> Pass the jelly, Kelly.

Independent, pair or guided work

- The children work in pairs, grouped so that a more confident writer is paired to support a less confident child.

- One child holds the writing plan with the chosen pair of words and supports their partner in typing their two words on to the sentence stem and adding a full stop when they have finished. Print out the sentence. (Refer to Resource Page C.)

- The pairs then reverse roles so that each child composes their own sentence by typing in their planned words. Guide where needed, but encourage a co-operative independent attempt.

- If you are working with a classroom computer rather than a computer suite, the children not using the computer can read *Pass the jam, Jim* (Resource Page A) in pairs, colouring capital letters red and full stops yellow. This will help reinforce punctuation.

Plenary

- Write simple sentences on the board for the class to read with you, making deliberate errors by missing out full stops or forgetting to put a capital letter for names, or at the start of a sentence.

- When you have written a sentence, ask the class to vote 'thumbs up' or 'thumbs down' to show whether it is a proper sentence.

- Challenge the children to tell you *why* it won't do as a sentence.

Writing Food Words

Objective

We will write our food words on the computer and use clipart

You need: Resource Page C; plastic play food; whiteboards; clipart or magazines of food pictures.

Word-level starter

- Hold up items of plastic food one by one. As you hold each one up, introduce the food by missing off the first sound in the word, for example:

- For each word the children correct you by supplying the missing first sound.

> Here we have a delicious piece of [b]read … [b]anana … [o]range … [c]ake …

- Adapt the game to support the phonic step that the children are currently being taught.

Whole class work

- Use the sentences that your class wrote in the previous lesson and challenge them to find the food word within their sentence.

- In supported composition, the children write their food word on individual whiteboards, checking that they have the right number of letters.

- Each child holds their whiteboard above their head and shouts out their word for the rest of the class to see.

Independent, pair or guided work

- Individually, the children type their words on to the computer as a class list of food words, using the same size and font as before.

- Work with a group to select and print clipart food pictures for a party picture.

- If you do not have access to a computer suite, the children not using the computer can draw a plate of their favourite foods, using 'have a go' writing to label the picture.

Plenary

- Discuss what has been learned about writing a sentence on the computer. Write down learning outcomes as a class checklist (see Resource Page C for ideas), to be displayed by the computer for future reference.

(**Pupil copymaster**)

Pass the jam, Jim

Hurry, Mabel, lay that table!
Jane, put Wayne back in his pram!
Where's the bread, Fred?
Bread I said, Fred.
Pass the jam, Jim,
Jam, Jim, jam.
Cut the cake, Kate,
Pour the tea, Lee.

Who wants cheese and who wants ham?
Pass the pot, Dot.
Is it hot, Dot?
Pass the jam, Jim,
Jam, Jim, jam.
Here's the salt, Walt.
Use your spoon, June.
Jill don't spill
And Phil don't cram!
What a mess, Bess,
On your dress, Bess.
Pass the jam, Jim,
Jam, Jim, jam.
Drink your juice, Bruce.
Slice of pie, Guy?
Sip your soup up slowly, Sam.
Who's for custard?
Where's the mustard?

Pass the jam, Jim,
Jam, Jim, jam.
Boil the kettle, Gretel,
Bring the butter, Betty.
Charles wants chips and so does Pam.
Thanks a lot, Jim …
Oh! You've NOT, Jim!
JIM! YOU'VE EATEN
ALL THE JAM!

Kate Umansky and Margaret Chamberlain

Pupil copymaster

Rhyming pair cards

ham	Sam
meat	Pete
pear	Clare
jelly	Kelly
cheese	Louise

(Exemplar material)

Checklist for writing a sentence on the computer

- Plan your sentence first

- Press the keys carefully, only once

- Use the space bar for word spaces

- Put a full stop at the end of a sentence

- To make capital letters, hold down the shift key

- Capital letters come at the start of a sentence and for names

- Click on the printer symbol to print

Marking ladder

In Foundation Stage Reception, work is likely to be assessed orally with the child, at the point of writing. The features identified as a checklist can be used to provide a focus and any comments recorded as a marking ladder.

Name: _____

Tick		Comment
	I planned my sentence.	
	I pressed the keys carefully.	
	I used the space bar for word spaces.	
	I used a full stop at the end of my sentence.	
	I used capital letters correctly.	
	I printed my sentence.	
	I can read my sentence back.	

Modern Poetry

Outcome

An imaginative poem with an identified structure and rhyme pattern

Objectives

Word

1 to understand and be able to rhyme through: recognising, exploring and working with rhyming patterns; extending these patterns by analogy, generating new and invented words in speech and spelling.

4 to link sounds and spelling patterns by using knowledge of rhyme to identify families of rhyming CVC words.

Text

10 to reread and recite rhymes with predictable and repeated patterns and experiment with similar rhyming patterns.

13 to think about and discuss what they intend to write, ahead of writing it.

14 to use experience of stories, poems and simple recounts as a basis for independent writing, e.g. retelling, substitution, extension, and through shared composition with adults.

Early learning goals

- Explore and experiment with words, sounds and texts.
- Use phonic knowledge to write simple regular words and phonetically plausible attempts at more complex words.
- Begin to form simple sentences, sometimes using punctuation.
- Enjoy listening to and using spoken and written language, and readily turn to it in play and learning.
- Listen with enjoyment and respond to rhymes and make up rhymes.
- Speak clearly and audibly, with confidence and control.

How you could plan this unit

Day 1	Day 1 (cont.)	Day 2	Day 3	Day 4
Personal experience Cross-curricular link to art. Visit an art exhibition, or look at pictures of famous paintings. Imagine you are inside the painting – what can you see/hear/smell? Close your eyes – imagine what happened before or after. Vocabulary: artist,	picture, painting, frame, use of senses, visible/ invisible	**Shared reading, drama**	**Shared reading**	**Shared reading and supported composition** Children explore finding rhyming pairs of words
		Invisible Pictures	*Identifying Rhymes*	

Day 5	Day 6
Planning for writing	**Shared writing**
Planning a Rhyme	*Writing a Rhyme*

Invisible Pictures

Objective

We will make 'pictures' using words and mime

You need: Resource Pages A and D; toy mouse or picture of mouse; stage block.

Word-level starter

- Play 'Squeak, mousie, squeak!' With the class sitting in a circle, pass a toy mouse around the circle to a child.

- *Each time we play the game, Mousie is going to squeak 'ee ee ee' in a different way.* The child who receives the mouse alters their voice to make Mousie squeak in the chosen way – high, low, scared, sleepy, happy, excited, quiet, loud.

- When Mousie has finished squeaking, the rest of the class reply with three squeaks to copy the voice pattern. Repeat with other children, who use different voices.

Whole class work

- Read the poem *Invisible Boy* (Resource Page A) with your class.

- Refer back to the previous lesson. Ask your class to identify what is different about the pictures you looked at yesterday and this picture of the invisible boy (which, of course, is blank!).

- Explain that poets can paint pictures too, by creating images using words. *Poets know that it is very important to choose the best words to paint these pictures. Without the words of the poem, we wouldn't know what was in the picture!*

- In pairs, the children can now mime the picture, taking it in turns to watch each other.

- Still working with their response partner, ask the children to describe exactly what they can see in the invisible picture. Prompt discussion through questions such as:
  - *What sort of house does the invisible boy live in?*
  - *Where does he keep his invisible mouse?*
  - *Can you describe the mouse?*

Independent, pair or guided work

- Working in supported groups, the children play 'Invisible pictures'. Standing on a stage block, the children take turns to act out a scenario from the scenario cards placed face down on the table (Resource Page D). The rest of the group try to guess the invisible picture from the mime.

- Ask the children to draw what *they* think the invisible boy and mouse looked like.

Plenary

- Response partners decide together on answers to the following questions:

> What does invisible mean?
>
> How is the poet painting an invisible picture for you?
>
> Can you paint your own invisible picture for your partner?

Identifying Rhymes

Objective

We will find out which lines of a poem rhyme and which do not

You need: Resource Pages A, B and F; plastic farm animals; a selection of poems from the class library.

Word-level starter

- Sitting in a big circle, pass a plastic animal around the circle to generate an oral rhyme string. Each child continues the rhyme string, adding their own rhyming word. Made-up words are allowed, as long as they rhyme, and the children can use a rhyme that has already been said. (Refer to Progression in Phonics, Step 2, Pebble game.)

- Start with simple CVC animals such as 'cat', 'dog', 'pig', 'hen'.

Whole class work

- Read through the poem *Invisible Boy* (Resource Page A) with your class again, encouraging them to join in as you point to the words, to demonstrate how the words you are reading match the words of the text (that is, one-to-one correspondence).

- Explain that poets sometimes use rhyme to make their poems sound good.

- ***Can anyone think of a poem or nursery rhyme that uses rhyme?*** The children discuss with response partners.

- With your class look again at the poem, referring to the exemplar analysis (Resource Page B).

Independent, pair or guided work

- In guided reading, read the frog poem (Resource Page F) and focus with your group on identifying rhyming words.

- Independent groups can read books from the class library collection, using a teaching assistant, classroom helper or paired reader from another class to support them in finding an example of a poem that uses rhyme.

Plenary

- Together, the class reviews the poems that have been found, putting them into two piles labelled 'These poems rhyme' and 'These poems do not rhyme'.

Planning a Rhyme

Objective

We will use new pairs of rhyming words to change a poem

You need: Resource Pages C and E; Blu-tack™; stage block.

Word-level starter

- Extend the challenge of the animal rhyme string by introducing animals with long vowel sounds: for example, 'mouse', 'sheep', 'goat', 'cow', and so on.

Whole class work

- Explain to the class that you are now going to plan your invisible picture poem, so that you know what you want to say before you write.

- Using the pairs of words on the rhyming pair cards (Resource Page E), model how these can be substituted for the words 'house' and 'mouse' to change the invisible picture that the poem paints.

- Point out that the rhyme pattern of this poem is lines 2 and 4, and 5 and 6.

- Use Blu-tack™ to add the new rhymes to the writing frame (Resource Page C) to change the poem, explaining that it is only the two key rhyming words on lines 2 and 4 that are changing the picture.

- Extend this investigation by choosing another word, but asking for suggestions for the rhyme. *Which words could we use for the rhyme at the end of line 4?*

- Choose one version, and explain why you have chosen it (because it paints a good picture with words, it makes you laugh, and so on).

- Model recording your plan in picture form, for example, draw a boy wearing a hat feeding a cat. Explain to your class that this plan will help you remember your rhymes for tomorrow.

Independent, pair or guided work

- Independently, each child draws a picture to plan the rhyme pair that they will use for their poem.

- Guided work could extend a high achieving group in attempting to write the two rhyming words under their picture.

Plenary

- Give the children the opportunity to present their picture plans to the class, standing on a stage block and holding up their picture for the rest of the class to try to guess the pair of rhymes.

- Write the pairs of words on the board as they are identified, to model the written representation.

- *Do all the words rhyme? Which is your favourite rhyme? Why?*

Writing a Rhyme

Objective

We will use new words to write our own version of the poem

You need: Resource Pages C and G; whiteboards and pens (one each); cardboard; dried pasta; gold paint.

Word-level starter

- Model writing on the board a full stop, a question mark and an exclamation mark, verbalising their formation. Identify their names and define their purpose with the class.

- *When I call out a name, decide which punctuation mark it is and draw it on your whiteboard.* Make sure that the board examples are clearly visible, to support the children's attempts. Make this a quick-fire game, moving swiftly between the three marks so that there are lots of chances to reinforce the learning.

Whole class work

- Model writing a new version of the poem with your class (Resource Page G), explaining the following:
  - capital letters at the start of lines of a poem
  - the rhyme pair at the end of lines 2 and 4, using the words from the children's picture plans from the previous lesson
  - the purpose of the punctuation (full stop, question mark, exclamation mark) – to help the reader put expression into the reading.

Independent, pair or guided work

- The children work in guided or independent groups to compose their new versions of the poem, changing the rhymes by using their picture plan.

- Support this composition as appropriate for the needs of each group through differentiated writing support: independent, writing frames (Resource Page C), scribed.

- Make ornate picture frames for the invisible pictures, cutting rectangular frames from cardboard, decorating with pasta and painting with gold paint. The poem can then be attached under the frame for display in an invisible art gallery.

Plenary

- Present the invisible poems in an assembly or to another class, to add a speaking and listening performance outcome.

(**Pupil copymaster**)

Invisible Boy

And here we see an invisible boy

In his lovely invisible house,

Feeding a piece of invisible cheese

To a little invisible mouse.

Oh, what a beautiful picture to see!

Will you draw an invisible picture for me?

Shel Silverstein

Classworks Literacy Year R © Julie Orrell, Nelson Thornes Ltd 2003

Exemplar analysis

Example of analysis of *Invisible Boy*

This is one of the words the poet has used that rhymes. Where does it come in the line? Rhyming words usually come at the end of lines. Can you think of any words that rhyme with 'house'?

What does the word 'invisible' mean? Which things are invisible in the poem? The poet is telling us that we will have to use our imagination to see the picture.

Here is the other rhyming word – 'mouse'. Let's say them really quickly together, to see if we can hear the rhyme – 'house, mouse, house, mouse, house, mouse'.

And here we see an <u>invisible</u> boy

In his lovely invisible <u>house</u>,

Feeding a piece of invisible cheese

To a little invisible <u>mouse</u>.

Oh, what a beautiful picture to <u>see</u>!

Will you draw an invisible picture for <u>me</u>?

Shel Silverstein

The poem ends with a question mark. This is a question mark (draw question mark). What does it mean? The poet is asking us if we will draw him an invisible picture, too.

There is another pair of rhyming words hiding in the poem – one is 'see'. Can we find its pair? Which part of a word sounds the same in a rhyme, is it the beginning or the end? Let's sound out the two words and see if we can hear that 'ee' sound at the end – 'see, me'.

Pupil copymaster

Writing frame for *Invisible Boy*

And here we see an invisible boy

In his lovely invisible _____ ,

Feeding a piece of invisible cheese

To a little invisible _____ .

Oh, what a beautiful picture to see!

Will you draw an invisible picture for me?

(Pupil copymaster)

Scenario cards

Feeding invisible milk to an invisible cat.	Cuddling an invisible baby who is crying.
Trying to stop an invisible crab pinching your toes.	Pressing the buttons in an invisible rocket to fly to an invisible planet.
Driving an invisible car on an invisible road.	Winding a large invisible snake around your neck.
Riding on the back of an invisible dolphin.	Painting an invisible picture with invisible paint.
Reading an invisible story to a friend.	Feeding an invisible dog an invisible bone.

Pupil copymaster

Rhyming pair cards

van	man
pen	hen
house	mouse
hat	cat
coat	goat
jeep	sheep

Pupil copymaster

A poem to read together

I am a hoppy little frog,

I'm green and brown with spots,

I live inside a hollow log,

I eat flies – lots and lots!

(Exemplar material)

Checklist and model for modern poetry

Example of a checklist for writing a poem ①

- Say it before we write it
- Hear and write sounds in words
- Paint invisible pictures with words
- Leave spaces between words
- Use capital letters at the start of lines
- Use rhyming words at the end of lines
- End the poem with a question

Example of modelled writing of new rhymes ②

And here we see an invisible boy
In his lovely invisible <u>coat</u>,
Feeding a piece of invisible cheese
To a little invisible <u>goat</u>.
And here we see an invisible boy
In his lovely invisible <u>hat</u>,
Feeding a piece of invisible cheese
To a little invisible …

(**Marking ladder**)

In Foundation Stage Reception, work is likely to be assessed orally with the child, at the point of writing. The features identified as a checklist can be used to provide a focus and any comments recorded as a marking ladder.

Name: _____

Tick		Comment
	I say it before I write it.	
	I can hear and write sounds in words.	
	I use a full stop at the end of a sentence.	
	I use capital letters correctly at the start of lines.	
	I put spaces in between words.	
	I use rhyming words at the end of lines.	
	I can generate a rhyme string.	
	I can read my new poem aloud.	

Classworks Literacy Year R © Julie Orrell, Nelson Thornes Ltd 2003

Instructions and Lists

Outcome

A list poem based on a shared text

Objectives

Word

10 [be taught] new words from their reading and shared experiences.

Sentence

3 [be taught] that words are ordered left to right and need to be read that way to make sense.

Text

11 through shared writing, to understand that writing can be used for a range of purposes, e.g. to send messages, record, inform, tell stories.

13 to think about and discuss what they intend to write, ahead of writing it.

15 to use writing to communicate in a variety of ways.

Early learning goals

- Use phonic knowledge to write simple regular words and phonetically plausible attempts at more complex words.
- Use talk to organise, sequence and clarify thinking, ideas, feelings and events.
- Show an understanding of how information can be found in non-fiction texts to answer questions about where, who, why and how.
- Use language to recreate roles and experiences.

How you could plan this unit

Day 1	Day 2	Day 3	Day 4	Day 5
Shared experience Bring in examples of lists: shopping, class register, recipes. Discuss common features and record. Use role-play area to guide experience of list-making. Make labels for food pictures cut from magazines and display as a word bank	**Shared reading**	**Reading and writing**	**Reading and writing**	**Planning and writing**
	A Pictorial List	*List of Ingredients*	*Planning to Write*	*Writing a List*

Day 6
Display Glue enlarged hippo templates (Resource Page E) to card. Sponge-paint grey. Using junk materials, stick 'ingredients' around hippo with bread top and bottom. Stick poems inside and tie with string. Display freestanding or hanging

A Pictorial List

Objective

We will make a list of food

You need: plastic food or pictures of food; carrier bag or basket; sandwich ingredients; magazines with food pictures; scissors; gluesticks.

Word-level starter

- Put your plastic food items into the bag or basket and explain that you are going to pull them out, one at a time. As you produce an item of food, your class rub their tummies and make the first sound that they can hear in the word in a 'hungry' voice, for example, marmalade = "mmmmmmm"; sausages = "sssssssssss", extending the sound as they rub their tummies.

- Use food to represent the sounds that the children are learning in their phonics work, encouraging them to identify the first phoneme that they can hear.

Whole class work

- *Can you describe what a sandwich is for someone who has never seen one? How would you make a sandwich?*

- In pairs, the children discuss answers. Take several answers for evaluation as a class, discussing and refining them.

- Demonstrate how to make a sandwich, explaining the ingredients and their functions.

- *What do you like inside your sandwiches?* Discuss sandwich fillings.

- List responses on the board, modelling the format of a list. Remind the children of the properties of lists that were identified as a checklist in the previous lesson.

Independent, pair or guided work

- The children cut out pictures from food magazines and stick to make a pictorial list of food. Remind them to stick food in a vertical line, as that is how lists are organised.

- With your guided group, help them to attempt to write down the sounds that they can hear next to their food pictures. Stretch the words out into very clear individual sounds with your voice to help them to hear all of the sounds in the word.

Plenary

- The children 'read' from their picture lists to their response partners the items of food they have found. This could be extended in role play – going shopping with a list.

List of Ingredients

Objective

We will make a shared list of ingredients for a hippo sandwich

You need: Resource Pages A, B and F; toy hippo or picture; whiteboards; highlighter pen; Blu-tack™.

Word-level starter

- Hold up the ingredients cards (Resource Page B) one by one, showing only the picture with the word covered. The class guess the first sound they can hear.

- You can differentiate this game to reflect the phonic stages the children have reached, for example, "Guess my last sound", "Guess my middle vowel".

Whole class work

- Refer back to the picture lists your class made in the previous lesson. Pretend that you have forgotten how to make a list. *Who can remember what makes a list different from a story?* Check responses against the checklist (Resource Page F).

- *Today we are not going to make just any old sandwich, but a very unusual and rather silly one. On the menu today is a hippo sandwich!*

- Check that your class know what a hippo is. In pairs, the children describe a hippo to each other. Prompt and extend discussion through open and closed questions:
  - *What colour is a hippo?*
  - *How big is a hippo?*
  - *What do you think hippos like doing all day?*
  - *Describe what a hippo's skin might feel like.*

- Use a toy hippo or picture of a hippo to review the answers to your questions.

- *If we were to write a recipe for a hippo sandwich, what could we include?* Model on the board some ingredients you might put in, recorded as a list:

bread
butter
sauce
tomato
hippo

Independent, pair or guided work

- Using whiteboards, the children work in pairs or a small guided group to note down some ingredients for a hippo sandwich, using have-a-go writing.

- Read the poem *Recipe for a Hippopotamus Sandwich* (Resource Page A).

- Discuss how poems can sometimes be about funny things, or nonsense. *Can you think of any nonsense poems or rhymes – things that are so silly they could not possibly be true?* Prompt the children to think of nursery rhymes, if necessary.

- Using a highlighter, the children come out and highlight items on the list of ingredients in the poem. Read each one as it is highlighted, modelling how you are working out what the word says by blending the sounds together to read.

- Point out that in recipes we need to know not just what to put in but also how much.

Plenary

- Use Blu-tack™ to stick the ingredients cards on to the board randomly. Ask the children to come out and rearrange the ingredient cards into a list.

- Revise *What makes a list?*

Planning to Write

Objective

We will plan a list of ingredients for our poem

You need: Resource Pages A–C (including enlarged versions of A and C, plus one per child); whiteboards.

Word-level starter

- Use the ingredients cards for bread, piece of string and pepper (Resource Page B). This time the objective is to move on from *hearing* the sound to *writing* the sound.

- Pair your class so that the children who are stronger in the transcriptional skills of spelling and handwriting are supporting those who are weaker.

- Show the pictures on the ingredients cards one at a time, giving the children time to discuss the first sound of each card and attempt to write it on their whiteboards, holding them up to show you.

- Encourage the children to support each other in this, by saying the movement of the letter as they write it. Both the children in each pair need to write the letter. The stronger partner will provide a model for the weaker to copy.

Whole class work

- Reread the poem with your class (Resource Page A), pointing to the words as you read and encouraging them to join in.

- Let the children's reading take over when you get to the list of ingredients. Point at the initial letter sound to give them a clue if they get stuck.

- Model how you are going to plan your own version of the poem. Use an enlarged copy of the planning frame (Resource Page C) and draw attention to the useful words box at the bottom.

- Scribe the ingredients you will use and the quantity word for each. As you plan, explain why you are making your choices and how you are using the word bank or the sounds in words to help you write them.

Independent, pair or guided work

- The children work independently or in guided groups to plan the ingredients and quantities they will use for their sandwich.

- Independently, the children write on their plans with the support of ingredients cards and word bank.

Plenary

- In pairs, your class read their plans to each other.

- Take a class vote on which is the silliest sandwich.

Writing a List

Objective

We will write a list poem giving instructions for making a hippo sandwich

You need: Resource Pages B, D (enlarged and individual) and F.

Word-level starter

- Complete the sequence: *identify sound → write letter → read* running through the previous lessons. Use the ingredients cards (Resource Page B) and this time cover up the picture, not the word. Challenge your class to read the words as you hold them up one at a time, as a flashcards game.

Whole class work

- ***Today we are going to use our writing plan from the last lesson to help us write our own poems.***

- Reread the ingredients plan and explain how you are now able to concentrate on the way you are writing your poem (the composition), as you have already decided what you want to say and how to write it in your plan.

- Read the beginning and ending of the poem on the writing frame (Resource Page D) and ask your class, **What is missing?** Answer: the list of ingredients.

- Write the list of ingredients from your plan into the frame, making the transfer explicit. As you write, model arranging your words vertically as a list.

- Return to the class checklist (Resource Page F) to remind your class of the features of list writing.

Independent, pair or guided work

- In independent time, the children write their recipes for a hippopotamus sandwich, using their plans to support them.

- Guide the children with weak handwriting skills by scribing their list for them. Then ask them to read back to you.

Plenary

- Place all of the poems flat on tables in the classroom, and do a 'walk and read' activity. The children are free to wander around the tables and read the poems that have been composed.

- Stop the action after they have read several poems, and ask them to turn to the person next to them and tell them about a poem that they liked, and what they particularly liked about it.

Pupil copymaster

Recipe for a Hippopotamus Sandwich

A hippo sandwich is easy to make.
All you do is simply take
One slice of bread,
One slice of cake,
Some mayonnaise,
One onion ring,
One hippopotamus,
One piece of string,
A dash of pepper –
That ought to do it.
And now comes the problem …
Biting into it!

Shel Silverstein

Classworks Literacy Year R © Julie Orrell, Nelson Thornes Ltd 2003

(Pupil copymaster)

Ingredients cards

bread	
cake	
mayonnaise	
onion ring	
hippopotamus	
piece of string	
pepper	

(Pupil copymaster)

Plan of ingredients

How many **?**   What **?**

_____   _____

_____   _____

_____   _____

_____   _____

_____   _____

Useful words

| cake | bread | pickle | sauce | jam |

| spoonful of | piece | slice | string |

| squirt | peanut butter | some | shake |

Number words

| one | two | three | four | five |

| six | seven | eight | nine | ten |

(Pupil copymaster)

Writing frame

RECIPE FOR A HIPPO SANDWICH

by _____

A hippo sandwich is easy to make.
All you do is simply take

_____

_____

_____

_____

That ought to do it.
And now comes the problem ...
Biting into it!

(**Pupil copymaster**)

Hippo template

(Exemplar material)

Checklist for lists

- They are written down the page, not across like a story

- They have no words joining them together

- They help us to remember things

- They might be in order

- They might tell us how many

Marking ladder

In Foundation Stage Reception, work is likely to be assessed orally with the child, at the point of writing. The features identified as a checklist can be used to provide a focus and any comments recorded as a marking ladder.

Name: _____

Tick		Comment
	I know what a list is.	
	I planned my writing.	
	I made a list.	
	I tried to write sounds in words.	
	I used useful words from the poem.	
	I can read my poem.	

Classworks Literacy Year R © Julie Orrell, Nelson Thornes Ltd 2003

Non-chronological Reports

Outcome

A non-chronological report – individual or group three-part zigzag book, based on a shared text

Objectives	**Word** **11** to make collections of personal interest or significant words and words linked to particular topics. **Sentence** **1** to expect written text to make sense and to check for sense if it does not. **Text** **1** through shared reading: to recognise printed and handwritten words in a variety of settings, e.g. labels, signs, notices; to understand and use correctly terms about books and print: 'book', 'cover', 'page', 'title'. **3** to reread a text to provide context clues to help read unfamiliar words. **11** through shared writing, to understand that writing can be used for a range of purposes, e.g. to send messages, record, inform, tell stories; to distinguish between writing and drawing in books and in own work. **12** through guided and independent writing, to write labels or captions for pictures and drawings. **13** to think about and discuss what they intend to write, ahead of writing it.
Early learning goals	• Show an understanding of how information can be found in non-fiction texts to answer questions about where, who, why and how. • Attempt writing for different purposes. • Find out about, and identify, some features of living things they observe. • Use their phonic knowledge to write simple regular words and make plausible attempts at more complex words. • Write labels and captions and begin to form simple sentences, sometimes using punctuation.
Note	• This unit has cross-curricular links to Early Learning Goals for exploration and investigation. If possible, support this unit by having tadpoles in the classroom, or visiting a pond to observe.

How you could plan this unit

Day 1	Day 1 (cont.)	Day 2	Day 3	Day 4
Shared experience Observe real tadpoles. Collect books about frogs. Discuss whether fiction or non-fiction. Sort into two piles. Identify difference and discuss: 'We read a non-fiction book when we want to find out about something.' In guided	reading, read a fiction and a non-fiction text and investigate differences. Ask children to look for books/pictures/models of frogs for class display	**Reading and writing** *First Sentence*	**Reading and writing** *Giving More Detail*	**Reading and writing** Introductory sentence for page 2 of class book (see Resource Pages C and D). Follow 'read, plan, write' format of Day 2. Use the sand tray with stones and pebbles to make a damp, shady environment that frogs would like to live in

Day 5	Day 6	Day 7	Day 8	Day 9
Reading and writing Second sentence for page 2 (see Resource Pages C and D). Explore in PE or drama how frogs move and the noises they make. Make models of worms and insects for the frogs to eat	**Reading and writing** Introductory sentence for page 3. Follow the 'read, plan, write' format of Day 2, using Resource Pages E and F. Observational drawings of tadpoles	**Reading and writing** Second sentence for page 3 (Resource Pages E and F). Make black silhouette tadpole pictures on pale blue backgrounds as a creative activity. This can provide a decorative cover page	**Reading and writing** *Writing Captions*	**Publishing** *Title Page*

157

First Sentence

Objective

We will write a short, factual sentence to explain what a frog is

You need: Resource Pages A, B and I; individual whiteboards; sample zigzag card book.

Sentence-level starter

- Write the sentence 'Frogs live on land and in the water', with each word on a different piece of card or whiteboard. (Include a card for the full stop.) Hand out the sentence cards to individual children, then arrange the children in a line to make a human sentence. Read the sentence together as a class. ***Does it make sense? A sentence is the way we write down an idea, so it has to make sense.***

- Ask your class to close their eyes, then you take one child out of the human sentence. Read the new sentence with the class. ***Which word is missing?*** If the children find this difficult, reread the sentence, pausing at the missing word. The children vote (thumbs up or thumbs down) as to whether it is a proper sentence.

- Repeat the game with a different missing word to help reinforce the concept of a sentence as a coherent idea.

Whole class work

- Explain that you are going to make books about frogs so that visitors to your classroom can use them to learn more about frogs. Show the format of a zigzag book. Explain that it will give lots of information for a frog pond display.

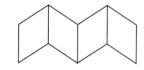

- Read *What is a frog?* (Resource Page A) with your class. Annotate the text with a marker pen to show the different parts – first sentence, picture, second sentence.

- Reread the first sentence and show that it answers the question 'What is a frog?' It does not give a full description, just a short, factual summary. Record this on a class checklist (see Resource Page I for ideas).

- Ask ***What is a frog?***. The children rehearse a short, factual answer in pairs. Take suggestions, and check against the checklist, revising where needed.

- Choose one of the suggestions and, using Resource Page B as a frame, model how you might write this idea as a sentence, for example:

> Frogs live near ponds.

As you write, explain what you are doing (see Resource Page I).

- Read the new sentence as a class, counting the words with claps and putting hands on heads to signify the full stop.

Independent, pair or guided work

- The children write their own first sentence, using Resource Page B as a frame. Differentiate support through 'have a go' independent writing, or a scribed group or individual sentence.

- The children illustrate the sentence with individual drawings or clipart pictures.

Plenary

- Ask the question ***What is a frog?*** Challenge the class to come up with 10 different (and appropriate) answers.

Giving More Detail

Objective

We will write a second sentence giving more detail

You need: Resource Pages A, B and I; a toy frog.

Word-level starter

- Play 'Pass the frog'. This game has a speaking and listening focus. Pass a toy frog around your class circle. As the frog reaches each child, it is their turn to speak and give a piece of factual information about frogs.

- Model how the game works by passing the frog to and fro between adults in the classroom to give examples:

> A frog breathes air … A frog can swim in the water … Frogs keep their skin moist … Frogs are amphibians.

- The children can repeat a frog fact.

Whole class work

- Read *What is a frog?* (Resource Page A) again with your class.

- Focus on the second and third sentence and discuss how they give further information.

- Look at your shared first sentence. ***Does it give us enough information?*** In pairs, ask the children to discuss what else we might need to know. ***Can you think of a factual sentence that will tell the reader more about frogs?*** Refer to examples from the starter game as a prompt.

- The children report their sentence back to the class.

- Record on the class checklist that the second sentence gives us further, more detailed information. (Refer to Resource Page I.)

- Model how you are going to take one of the ideas and use it to write your second sentence, underneath the picture on the writing frame (Resource Page B).

- Read the new, modelled sentence with your class, checking that it adds information.

Independent, pair or guided work

- Support the children in writing a second, more detailed sentence.

Plenary

- Consolidate the understanding of a sentence as an idea that makes sense on its own by playing 'Sensible sentences'. Challenge your class to spot which sentences make sense, and which have something missing. Read the sentences below one at a time, giving your class enough time to repeat it to themselves and agree with a partner how to vote. They can vote either by 'thumbs up, thumbs down', through yes/no response cards or by putting a tick or a cross on their whiteboards.

> Frogs like to swim in the.
>
> Frogs keep their skin moist.
>
> Frogs live the land.
>
> Frogs amphibians.

- Challenge your class to explain to you *why* 1, 3 and 4 are not sentences.

Writing Captions

Objective

We will write captions for our pictures

You need: Resource Page G; gluesticks.

Word-level starter

- Follow the pattern of the game 'Squeak, piggy, squeak!'. One child sits in the middle of the circle with their eyes closed. Another child is chosen to be the 'frog' and make the noise 'ribbit ribbit' in a specified way – high, low, squeaky, growly and so on. The child in the middle has to focus on where the sound is coming from and point to that area to try to guess the frog.

- Extend and vary the game by using the phonemes that the class is learning in their phonics work.

Whole class work

- Read the three completed pages of the book that you have modelled for the class.

- Review against the class checklist, making sure that the information is factual, concise and divided into introductory and secondary information.

- Ask your class to read one page themselves, or to a partner. *Is there anything that we have missed out?*

- Draw attention to the fact that on the picture there are little labels, or captions. Read the captions together, and discuss their function. Add to the checklist that captions name parts of the picture.

- In relation to your modelled text, ask your class to discuss what would be a good caption for one of the pictures.

- Select an appropriate caption from the word bank (Resource Page G) to represent a suggestion, or scribe a new one.

- Show how you can then stick this on to the picture to tell the reader what it is.

Independent, pair or guided work

- The children choose an appropriate caption for one of their pictures and glue it on.

Plenary

- Challenge the children to look through non-fiction books from the school or class library collection to try to find another book with captions.

Title Page

Objective

We will write a title page for our book

You need: Resource Page H; a selection of library books; magnetic letters; thick paper for zigzag books; gluesticks; decorative tadpole paper from earlier lesson.

Word-level starter

- Use magnetic letters to demonstrate how to segment in order to spell the word 'frogs'. Sound out the word slowly, one phoneme at a time and show the children how you are selecting the letter to represent each sound.

- Muddle up the magnetic letters on the board into various combinations for your class to solve. Model how to solve the first word challenge, by sounding out the word 'frogs' and identifying the first phoneme. Continue for the rest of the word.

- Challenge the children to sound out the word 'frogs' to help solve further combinations.

- If you have any children who are capable of tackling CVC words, differentiate this activity by giving them whiteboards to solve the challenge independently.

Whole class work

- Using a selection of books, discuss the front covers, asking the children to identify what information is on the cover. Identify the title and author.

- Display Resource Page H. **What has the author chosen as a title for the text on frogs?** Refer to the word-level starter, and the investigation of the word 'frogs'. Look at the title word together, sounding it out and checking that the author has got it right.

- On whiteboards, challenge the children to 'have a go' at writing the word 'frogs', encouraging them to sound out the word and put down the sounds that they know.

- Identify that the author is the person who has written the book. **Who is the author of your book?** On whiteboards, the children write their names.

- You may wish to discuss the role of the contents page in summarising information in a non-fiction book (see Resource Page H).

- Model how you write the title 'Frogs' and your name as author as a title page.

Independent, pair or guided work

- The children compose their title pages on the tadpole paper made previously.

- Encourage independent writers to write the word 'frogs' themselves, supporting with the shared text cover.

- Use magnetic letters on a small board to work as a group with any children not yet writing independently and consolidate the word-level activity with them to spell the word 'frogs'. Photocopy the magnetic letters as a title strip for each member of the group to colour and stick on their title page.

- Publish the zigzag books by sticking the title page on the first section of folded card, then the other pages in order.

Plenary

- In paired reading partners, the children read their completed books to each other.

- Display the published books in a 'Finding out about frogs' pond display.

Pupil copymaster

Page 1

What is a frog?

Frogs live on land and in water.

Frog

Soft, moist skin

Creatures that live on land and in water are called amphibians. All amphibians breathe air and have soft, moist skin.

1

(Pupil copymaster)

Page 1 writing frame

What is a frog?

1

Pupil copymaster

Page 2

Adult frogs

Frogs live in damp places. Damp shady homes help to keep the frog's skin moist.

Damp shady home

The frog hops to move around. Frogs eat worms, beetles and other insects.

2

Pupil copymaster

Page 2 writing frame

Adult frogs

2

Page 3

Frog babies

Frogs lay their eggs in the water.

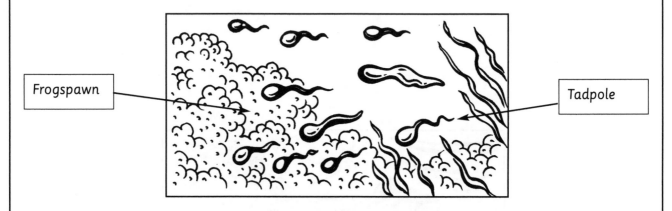

Frogspawn

Tadpole

Each egg is inside a jelly-ball, called frogspawn. Inside each jelly-ball a little tadpole starts to grow. After ten days the tadpole swims out. Tadpoles eat little water plants. Tadpoles change into frogs.

3

Classworks Literacy Year R © Julie Orrell, Nelson Thornes Ltd 2003

Page 3 writing frame

Frog babies

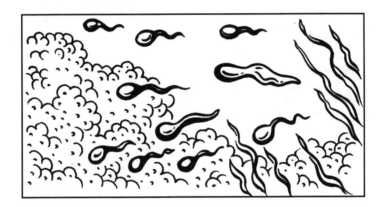

3

(Pupil copymaster)

Caption word bank

frogspawn	pond
water	stone
grass	shady home
adult frog	skin
worm	beetle
insect	eyes
tadpole	jelly-ball

PHOTOCOPIABLE · PHOTOCOPIABLE ·

Pupil copymaster

A contents page

FINDING OUT ABOUT FROGS

Contents

(Exemplar material)

Checklists for non-chronological reports

Example of a checklist for writing a first sentence

- Start with a capital letter

- Form each letter carefully so that the reader can understand what you have written

- Sound out each word to help you spell

- Leave a finger space between words to stop them getting muddled up together

- Count the words to make sure your written sentence matches your planned idea

- Put a full stop at the end of the sentence to show that this is the end of this idea

Example of a checklist for a non-chronological report

- Non-fiction books give us information

- The first sentence gives us a short, factual statement, answering the reader's question

- There is usually a photograph, or a picture

- The second sentence gives us more detail, explaining its qualities

- The pictures have captions to label important parts

- The title page tells us what the book is called and who wrote it

Marking ladder

In Foundation Stage Reception, work is likely to be assessed orally with the child, at the point of writing. The features identified as a checklist can be used to provide a focus and any comments recorded as a marking ladder.

Name: _____

Tick		Comment
	My book gives information.	
	My book answers questions.	
	I have used captions.	
	I can write my name as author.	
	I have given my book a title.	

Fairy Tales

Outcome

A class book of stories retelling The Three Billy-goats Gruff

Objectives

Word

10 [be taught] new words from their reading and shared experiences.

Sentence

1 to expect written text to make sense and to check for sense if it does not.

2 to use awareness of the grammar of a sentence to predict words during shared reading and when rereading familiar stories.

Text

2 to use a variety of cues when reading: knowledge of the story and its context, and awareness of how it should make sense grammatically.

5 to understand how story book language works and to use some formal elements when retelling stories.

7 to use knowledge of familiar texts to re-enact or retell to others, recounting the main points in correct sequence.

12 through guided and independent writing, to experiment with writing and recognise how their own version matches and differs from conventional version.

13 to think about and discuss what they intend to write, ahead of writing it.

Early learning goals

- Extend vocabulary, exploring the meaning and sounds of new words.
- Explore and experiment with words, sounds and texts.
- Use phonic knowledge to write simple regular words and phonetically plausible attempts at more complex words.
- Use talk to organise, sequence and clarify thinking, ideas, feelings and events.
- Use language to recreate roles and experiences.
- Retell narratives in the correct sequence, drawing on language patterns of stories.

How you could plan this unit

Day 1	Day 2	Day 3	Day 4	Day 5
Shared reading Read several fairy tales, and identify key common features: fairy tales are not true; often set a long time ago; have unusual characters and settings. Begin a class checklist (see Resource Page F for ideas)	**Shared reading, drama, talk for writing** Make a list of phrases: 'Once upon time, there lived …'; 'Long, long ago'; 'deep dark forest'; 'happily ever after'. Turn play area into a 'fairy tale forest' and display phrases. Guided play: adventures in forest	**Talk for writing** *A Story Sandwich*	**Shared reading** *The Three Billy-goats Gruff* (Resource Page B). Refer to story sandwich and use marker pen to identify story parts: start, problem, events, resolution, end. The children use chunks of text and in guided groups stick them together to recreate story	**Drama, talk for writing** Guided groups act out *The Three Billy-goats Gruff*. Use drama to develop understanding of character, sequence and language. If appropriate, ask a parent to video the drama to review as plenary. Discuss what helped to make a good tale

Day 6	Day 7	Day 8	Day 9
Shared writing *Starting a Story*	**Shared writing** *Developing the Story*	**Shared writing** *Resolving the Story*	**Shared writing** Story ending. Identify typical 'happy ending' (bottom slice of bread in sandwich). Explore possible words and phrases to model your own version of ending to the class. The children write their own story endings in supported composition

A Story Sandwich

Objective

We will put the parts of a story in order

You need: Resource Page A (one per child, plus enlarged version); a hat; scissors; gluesticks; Blu-tack™.

Word-level starter

- Play 'Silly sentences'. Focus on developing awareness of the first sound in a word (*Progression in Phonics* Step 2, Jingles). The children work in pairs to generate a 's' word to complete the sentences:

> Sally saw some silly ...
> Sam the snake started to ...
> Silver spaceman saw a ...

- Play 'I made a sandwich and I used ...' game using the phoneme s̲. With your class sitting in a circle, start the game by stressing the s̲ sound in 's̲andwich'. In turn, the children add a further food word to the silly sandwich, for example, 'sausage', 'salami', 'sweets', 'spinach', 'sweetcorn', and so on.

Whole class work

- Demonstrate to your class how a story circle works. Pass a 'story hat' around the circle. Each child wears it in turn.

- As the hat moves from child to child, tell the well-known fairy tale of *Goldilocks and the Three Bears*. Identify the different parts of the story – start, problem, events, resolution, ending – as the story develops.

- Using a different fairy tale, for example, *Little Red Riding Hood*, encourage your class to try to make a new story circle. When it is their turn to wear the hat, they add the next bit of the story. Celebrate the use of appropriate language and structure in order to exemplify features of the genre.

- Share the concept that stories are a bit like building a sandwich. Using an enlarged copy of the story sandwich, demonstrate cutting up the sandwich into its constituent parts and then re-assembling it.

Independent, pair or guided work

- The children use copies of the story sandwich (Resource Page A), cut into five strips.

- Working in pairs, they build their sandwich and stick the sandwich together once they have agreed the order.

Plenary

- Using Blu-tack™, stick the paper sandwich to the whiteboard, in the wrong order.

- In pairs, the children discuss with their response partner what the order should be.

- One pair explains why the order is wrong and rearranges the sandwich to give the original order – start, problem, events, resolution, ending.

- Repeat, starting with a different wrong order.

Starting a Story

Objective

We will write a good story start, using fairy tale language

You need: Resource Pages B, E and F; computer (optional).

Word-level starter

- Model the formation of the three letters 'l', 'm', 'b' on the board, showing the starting point and direction of movement and linking graphemes to their sounds.

- Encourage your class to try these letters in 'skywriting' – drawing them in the air with their fingers. Use a 'patter' to verbalise the movement of the letter as you are forming it (see *Developing Early Writing*).

- Play a quick-fire game using whiteboards where you call out one of the three sounds and the children draw it on their whiteboard, then hold it up to show each other. Highlight examples of correct formation.

Whole class work

- With your class, reread the first two paragraphs representing the start of the story of *The Three Billy-goats Gruff* (Resource Page B).

- Model writing your own version for the class (see Resource Page E), exemplifying the following and linking to the story sandwich model:
  - the fairy-tale language at the start – 'Once upon a time'
  - introduction of the characters: the three goats – Little, Middle and Big. Refer back to the word-level starter. *These are the sounds we practised earlier.*
  - where do they want to go?
  - why do they want to go there?
  - introduction of the Troll; description of the Troll; where does he live?

> 'Once upon a time' = bread of story sandwich
>
> description of Troll = egg of story sandwich

- Represent the key points as a class checklist for independent work (see Resource Page F for ideas).

- Working in pairs, the children rehearse their story start with their response partner. *Have they managed to include the points identified on the checklist?*

Independent, pair or guided work

- Using the word bank from an earlier lesson for support, ask the children to write their story starts in 'have a go' writing. Differentiate the support as appropriate, for example, as a guided group story start composed on the computer and printed out for the children.

Plenary

- Read several children's story starts with the class and identify checklist features.

Developing the Story

Objective

We will develop our story by showing what happens next

You need: Resource Pages C and E; magnetic letters.

Word-level starter

- Using magnetic letters, put the words 'trip' and 'trap' on the board.

- In pairs, challenge the children to sound out the words. Explain that there are four sounds in each word to identify.

- Play 'Missing sounds'. Remove a letter from one of the words while the children's eyes are closed and ask them to decide with their partner which sound is missing. Differentiate your questions to challenge the children to tell you the missing phoneme by sounding out the word and identifying what is missing.

> _rip   tri_   tr_p   t_ip

- ***What is the same about the two words?*** Explain that it is only the short vowel that has changed.

- Chant the refrain 'TRIP TRAP, TRIP TRAP, TRIP TRAP', encouraging the children to find the rhythm of the words by patting their knees or nodding their heads from side to side.

Whole class work

- Reread the next section of the story (Resource Page C) with your class.

- Model writing your own version of the development (see Resource Page E). As you write, point out the following:
  - who went first?
  - use of capitals for the noise to tell the reader to make it LOUD!
  - the rhythm of TRIP TRAP, TRIP TRAP.
  - the Troll's threat. Use of speech marks to tell the reader that someone is talking.
  - the trick that the goats are playing on the Troll.

> this section = cheese of story sandwich

Independent, pair or guided work

- The children continue to write their stories, supported as in the previous lesson.

Plenary

- Pretend that you are the horrible, hungry Troll who lives under the bridge. ***Now I'm coming to gobble you up!*** Ask your class to read the name of the goat that you write on the board (Little/Middle/Big) and act the response of the little, middle or big goat to your refrain.

Resolving the Story

Objective

We will solve the problem in our story

You need: Resource Pages D and E; whiteboards.

Word-level starter

- Play a 'Big Billy-goat Gruff' game. Hold up phoneme cards one by one to reflect the sounds that the class has been learning in their phonics work. The children say the sounds that you show them in a Big Billy-goat Gruff voice, a 'rough, roaring' voice.

- Explore the alliteration of 'rough, roaring' by finding other alliterative voices, for example, 'sweet, smiling'/'fierce, furious'/'smooth, silky'.

- Write the alliterative words on the board to demonstrate that they have the same letter at the start.

Whole class work

- Reread the next section of the text (Resource Page D).

- Model the resolution of the story for the class (see Resource Page E). Explain the use of:
  - alliteration for the Troll – 'horrible and hungry'
  - alliteration also for the goat's voice – 'fierce and furious'
  - the connective 'then' to show the order of events
  - the word 'but' at the start of the sentence that builds up the drama
  - the word 'butted' to describe how the troll was thrown off the bridge – goats butt
  - onomatopoeia with the word 'splash' to describe the noise that the Troll made. Discuss other noise words that you could use, for example, 'wheeeee', 'crash', 'bang', 'splat'.

> this section = tomato of story sandwich

- With response partners, the children orally rehearse what they are going to write. They plan alliteration to represent Big Billy-goat's voice, and a good word to describe the sound of the Troll as he falls in the river. This can be recorded on whiteboards in supported composition.

Independent, pair or guided work

- The children write the resolutions to their Troll problems, supported as before.

Plenary

- Make a collection of good examples of onomatopoeic words and display as a 'noisy' mobile.

- Refer back to the story sandwich model and count the parts of the sandwich that have already been built.

PHOTOCOPIABLE PHOTOCOPIABLE

(Pupil copymaster)

A story sandwich

Story start

Who, what, where, when, why?

Something happens

Things are sorted out

Story end

(Pupil copymaster)

The Three Billy-goats Gruff – story start

Once upon a time three billy-goats lived together in a field on a hillside. Their names were Big Billy-goat Gruff, Middle Billy-goat Gruff and Little Billy-goat Gruff.

A river ran beside the billy-goats' field, and one day they decided to cross it, to eat the grass on the other side. But first they had to go over the bridge, and under the bridge lived a great ugly Troll.

Classworks Literacy Year R © Julie Orrell, Nelson Thornes Ltd 2003

Pupil copymaster

The Three Billy-goats Gruff – continued

First Little Billy-goat Gruff stepped on to the bridge.
TRIP TRAP, TRIP TRAP, went his hoofs.

"Who's that tripping over my bridge?" roared the Troll.

"It is only I, Little Billy-goat Gruff, going across the river to make myself fat," said Little Billy-goat Gruff, in such a small voice.

"Now I'm coming to gobble you up," said the Troll.

"Oh please don't eat me, I'm so small," said Little Billy-goat Gruff. "Wait for the next billy-goat, he's much bigger."

"Well, be off with you," said the Troll.

A little while later, Middle Billy-goat Gruff stepped on to the bridge.

TRIP TRAP, TRIP TRAP, went his hoofs.

"Who's that tripping over my bridge?" roared the Troll.

"It is only I, Middle Billy-goat Gruff, going across the river to make myself fat," said Middle Billy-goat Gruff, whose voice was not so small.

"Now I'm coming to gobble you up," said the Troll.

"Oh no, don't eat me," said Middle Billy-goat Gruff. "Wait for the next billy-goat, he's the biggest of all."

"Very well, be off with you," said the Troll.

PHOTOCOPIABLE PHOTOCOPIABLE

Pupil copymaster

The Three Billy-goats Gruff – ending

It wasn't long before Big Billy-goat Gruff sped on to the bridge.

TRIP TRAP, TRIP TRAP, TRIP TRAP, went his hoofs and the bridge groaned under his weight.

"Who's that tramping over my bridge?" roared the Troll.

"It is I, Big Billy-goat Gruff," said Big Billy-goat Gruff, who had a rough roaring voice of his own.

"Now I'm coming to gobble you up," said the Troll, and at once he jumped on to the bridge, immensely horrible and hungry.

But Big Billy-goat Gruff was very fierce and strong. He put down his head and charged the Troll and butted him so hard he flew high into the air and then fell down, down, down, splash into the middle of the river. And the great ugly Troll was never seen again.

Then Big Billy-goat Gruff joined Middle Billy-goat Gruff and Little Billy-goat Gruff in the field on the far side of the river. There they got so fat that they could hardly walk home again, and if the fat hasn't fallen off them, they're still fat now.

So snip, snap, snout, this tale's told out!

(Exemplar material)

Modelled writing

Beginning

Once upon a time, there lived three billy-goats.

They were called Big Billy-goat, Middle Billy-goat and Little Billy-goat.

They wanted to cross the river to eat the green, green grass.

Under the bridge lived a great ugly Troll. He was horrible and he was hungry!

Developing

Little Billy-goat went first.

TRIP TRAP, TRIP, TRAP went his hoofs.

"Who's that tripping over my bridge? I'm coming to gobble you up!" roared the Troll. "Wait for the next billy-goat — he's much bigger," squeaked the little one, in a tiny voice. TRIP TRAP, TRIP TRAP, Middle Billy-goat played the same trick on the Troll.

Resolving

Then it was Big Billy-goat's turn. The Troll jumped on to the bridge, horrible and hungry. But Big Billy-goat was very big and very strong. "It is I!" he said, in a fierce, furious voice. He butted the Troll up in the air and off the bridge he flew with a splash!

Ending

The three billy-goats crossed the bridge safely to the field and munched green, green grass happily ever after. As for the great ugly Troll, he was never seen again.

PHOTOCOPIABLE · PHOTOCOPIABLE

(Exemplar material)

Checklist for fairy tales

- Use fairy tale language

- Start with 'Once upon a time'

- Describe the characters

- Tell the reader details – who? what? where? when? how?

- Show the problem!

- Solve the problem

- Use noise words – onomatopoeia

- Use alliteration

- Make it a happy ending

(**Marking ladder**)

In Foundation Stage Reception, work is likely to be assessed orally with the child, at the point of writing. The features identified as a checklist can be used to provide a focus and any comments recorded as a marking ladder.

Name: _____

Tick		Comment
	I used fairy tale language.	
	I made a story sandwich.	
	I described my characters.	
	I tried to hear and write sounds in words.	
	I used a 'noisy' word.	
	I used alliteration.	
	I can tell my story in sequence.	
	I can read my story.	

Marking ladder

Name: _____

Tick		Comment

Classworks Literacy Year R © Julie Orrell, Nelson Thornes Ltd 2003